AF000382

THE FUGGEREI
A Social Home Since 1521

1

2

3

4

What does the Fuggerei mean to you as an Augsburg citizen?

"It is a cultural enrichment in every respect and a tourist attraction, but also a landmark of the city. I think, Augsburg without the Fuggerei is like trying to eat a salad and there's no dressing."

Augsburg citizen

SERVICE

TIPS FOR YOUR VISIT

ACCESSIBILITY

Due to its historical architecture, the Fuggerei is not completely accessible for handicapped individuals. However, we are constantly striving to improve accessibility. Except for the museum in the (former) air-raid shelter, all museums are accessible via ramps for people with impaired mobility. Nonetheless, there are thresholds in the historical flat so that individual rooms are only accessible with assistance.

The media stations in the museums are accessible for individuals who use a wheelchair. The subtitling in the media stations makes visiting the museums also suitable for the hearing impaired. In addition, we offer guided tours especially for individuals with hearing impairments. Those tours of the Fuggerei are held in German sign language.

For people with visual impairments, we generally recommend visiting the Fuggerei with an accompanying person, as the site is difficult to explore independently. Individual elements in our exhibitions, such as a tactile model of the Fuggerei or audio stations, enable visitors to experience the Fuggerei haptically and audio-visually.

PLEASE BE CONSIDERATE

The Fuggerei residents appreciate your interest in the Fuggerei, but also your respect for their privacy.

Please do not ring doorbells, look curiously into ground floor windows, or take pictures of residents without their permission. A polite greeting, on the other hand, is always welcome.

DOGS

Dogs are allowed in the Fuggerei but must be kept on a leash. You will find dog toilets in the green area near the (former) air-raid shelter and in the park

EMERGENCIES

In case of an emergency, please ask the cashier at the ticket office. The fire extinguisher and a defibrillator are located to the left of the ticket office in the entrance area. Otherwise, please dial 112.

SERVICE

ADDRESS

Fürstlich und Gräflich
Fuggersche Stiftungen
Fuggerei 56, 86152 Augsburg

OPENING HOURS

April to September – 9 a.m. to 8 p.m.
October to March – 9 a.m. to 6 p.m.

HOW TO EXPLORE THE FUGGEREI

To not miss out on anything, it is recommended to follow the tour described in this guide. It takes you to various points of interest along the alleyways and explains unique details of the Fuggerei. Also discover the four museums with exciting insights into everyday life then and now. → DURATION: approx. 1 hour

GUIDED TOURS

We offer general and several themed tours. Booking and further information at:
→ www.fugger.de

NEW, FAST AND EXCITING

Experience the Fuggerei on Facebook, Instagram and YouTube

Alexander Count Fugger-Babenhausen
Chairman of the Princely and Comital Fugger Family Senior Council

DEAR VISITORS AND EVERYONE INTERESTED IN THE FUGGEREI,

From the very beginning, the Fuggerei was something special, much more than just a roof over one's head. The place itself, the size, the architecture, but above all the social approach went beyond anything known at the time of its inception. Fellow citizens in need are supported by affordable and adequate housing. In return, they pay a small monetary contribution and say three prayers a day. Therefore, the residents of the Fuggerei were and are not merely recipients of charity but lead a self-determined life in dignity here. Thus, the Fuggerei is a social home and provides targeted help for self-help. In this way, it has contributed to social cohesion for half a millennium. This humanistic idea is part of the foundational concept of the Fuggerei and is supposed to live on forever.

After all, Jakob Fugger wanted his descendants to ensure the continuity of Fuggerei "for all eternity". As a family, we take this responsibility very seriously and have been executing the founder's will in accordance with the charter of foundation of 1521 for many generations. This illustrates that the initial idea can indeed be transferred into the future. With the Fuggerei NEXT500 Project, we therefore want to share our experiences and start a conversation about how more social living spaces can be created along the lines of the Fuggerei. Affordable housing is one of the greatest social challenges of our time. At the same time, we are strengthening the Fuggerei here in Augsburg as well as its original idea.

As visitors, friends, and supporters, you make an essential contribution to the recognition and continuity of the Fuggerei. Stay connected to this unique social home and its people. For this, I thank you most sincerely on behalf of the Family Senior Council, the administration, and all residents.

DID YOU KNOW?

SEVEN IMPORTANT ANSWERS

WHEN WAS THE FUGGEREI FOUNDED?

Jakob Fugger had the first Fuggerei houses built in 1516. The first families moved in the same year. Until completion in 1523, other residents gradually followed. However, Jakob Fugger did not officially establish the foundation until 1521 in a so-called charter of foundation. This is the reason why the 23rd of August 1521 is considered the "birthday" of the Fuggerei.

WHAT DOES "THE OLDEST SOCIAL SETTLEMENT IN THE WORLD" MEAN?

Charitable housing for the poor existed even before the Fuggerei. But it is the oldest social housing complex that has been in continuous existence to this day. Apart from two brief periods of destruction during the Thirty Years' War and the Second World War, people in need have always lived here.

WHO LIVES IN THE FUGGEREI?

On average, 150 people live in the social housing complex project today. Couples, families, and individuals in need, who have lived in Augsburg for at least two years and are of Catholic faith, are accepted as residents. Age, origin, or gender do not play a role in admission.

DID YOU KNOW?

88 CENT RENT

3 PRAYERS PER DAY

HOW "MUCH" IS THE RENT?

As stipulated in the charter of foundation from 1521, the consideration for a Fuggerei flat still consists of three prayers a day, which each resident is to say for the salvation of the founder's and his family's souls, and one guilder a year — the equivalent of 88 cents annual rent, plus 88 cents a year for the Fuggerei priest. In addition, the residents pay for utilities, electricity, and heating.

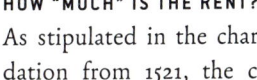

FOUNDATION FOREST

TOURISM

HOW IS THE FUGGEREI FUNDED?

To this day, the basis for funding the Fuggerei are the foundation assets that Jakob Fugger contributed and that were increased by his successors. Initially, the money was invested at interest, and from 1660 onwards in real estate and forest. The revenue from the foundation's forest is still the main source of income for running the Fuggerei today, in addition to the important income from admission fees and rental income from real estate property.

DID YOU KNOW?

WHO IS RESPONSIBLE FOR THE FUGGEREI?

Jakob Fugger had no children; this is why he left the responsibility for his foundations to the descendants of his brothers. Today, there are three lines of the Fugger family, each of which sends a representative to the Princely and Comital Fugger Family Senior Council. This body operates on a strategic decision-making level for the Fugger Foundations on an honorary basis. The administrator, together with his team, is responsible for the implementation of their decisions and the day-to-day business: from the foresters to the accounting department.

WHO OWNS THE FUGGEREI?

As a foundation, the Fuggerei belongs only to itself, not to the Fugger family, not to the city, and not to the state. The foundation's assets must be preserved for all eternity – as far as possible – for the fulfilment of the foundation's purpose. This means that the income from the foundation must be used to ensure the continued existence of the Fuggerei as a social settlement for people in need. This is the responsibility of the Fugger Family.

A TIMELESS IDEA: LIVING FOR DIGNITY

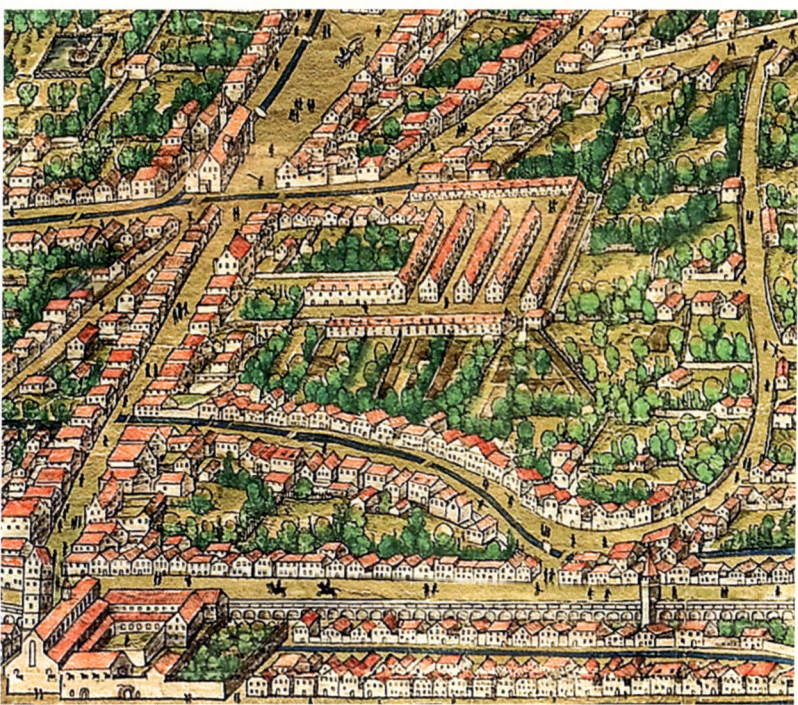

The Fuggerei is clearly visible on this plan by goldsmith Jörg Seld from 1521. The complex was still under construction at the time. Jakob Fugger had continuously acquired plots of land in Jakobervorstadt for his social housing complex from 1514 onwards. In 1516, the construction of the terraced houses began under the direction of master builder Thomas Krebs. In 1523, the complex with 52 houses as well as administration and stable buildings was completed as planned. There was room for about 300 to 350 people: poor craftsmen and day laborers with their families, who were able to make ends meet thanks to the low rent and thus could lead an independent life in dignity. The Fuggerei finally reached its current dimensions with 67 houses when it was expanded in the 19th and 20th century after the Second World War.

ENTRANCE AREA
Senior Council Building
Administration Building
Markusplätzle (St. Mark's Square)
Höchstetter Erker

ENTRANCE AREA

OPEN THE GATES TO THE HEART OF THE FUGGEREI

The Senior Council Building

The original Fuggerei already closed off to the north with a house and stables on Jakoberstraße. In 1548, this so-called "front dwelling" was converted into the administrator's house with a gateway. Since then, this has been the main entrance to the Fuggerei. Today's building, however, originates from the time after the Second World War.

The Fuggerei was severely damaged during an air raid in 1944. More than two thirds of the buildings had to be rebuilt – including the gate building at the entrance. Today, the upper floor is used for conferences and the meetings of the Princely and Comital Fugger Family Senior Council; hence the name "Senior Council Building".

The Fugger Family Senior Council meets in the conference room. Guests are received here and meetings with external participants are being held in this room as well.

ENTRANCE AREA

The restaurant "Die Tafeldecker" on the ground floor is open to guests all year round.

Delicious dining

Jakob Fugger watches the guests when they are dining deliciously: In the Fuggerei restaurant, you can enjoy seasonal, Bavarian-Swabian specialties with an international twist. In the summer months and around Christmas, the beer garden is also open for a secluded treat. Menu and further information at:

→ **www.dietafeldecker.de**

ENTER HERE

There are four main gates and two side entrances to the Fuggerei. For visitors, the gate on Jakoberstraße is the only entrance today. Residents, however, can also use all the other gates during the day. Between 10 p.m. and 4.30 a.m., all entrances are closed. A night watchman then opens the gate in Ochsengasse for residents (page 64).

ENTRANCE AREA

Informative: the founder's plaques

The stone tablet and the coat of arms stones with the Fugger lilies above the gate are historically documented. They were already present in the early Fuggerei and were integrated during the reconstruction. Two further plaques with an identical Latin text can be found above the gates to Saugasse and Ochsengasse.

THE LATIN TEXT TRANSLATES AS:

"1519: The brothers Ulrich, Georg, and Jakob Fugger from Augsburg, who are convinced that they were born for the benefit of this city and feel obliged to return to it their fortune received from the highest and most benevolent God, have out of piety and as an example of magnanimous generosity given, donated, and dedicated 106 dwellings with all facilities to their righteous but poor fellow citizens."

INTERESTING

➜ In 1519, the Fuggerei was still under construction, but the first houses were already inhabited. Jakob Fugger's brothers were already deceased at the time, but he still expressly established the foundation in their name. By doing so, he strengthened the commemoration and honor of the Fugger family.

➜ The idea that no goods could be obtained without God's help and that something had to be given back in return was the conviction of the time. Jakob Fugger also expressed this conviction on other occasions.

➜ The foundation of the Fuggerei "in exemplum", which means "as an example", still plays an important role today. For the 500th anniversary of the Fuggerei in 2021, a completely new idea was introduced with the Fuggerei NEXT500 project: Founders worldwide can now implement the core social idea of the Fuggerei and found new, individual social housing projects inspired by the Fuggerei (page 84 - 87).

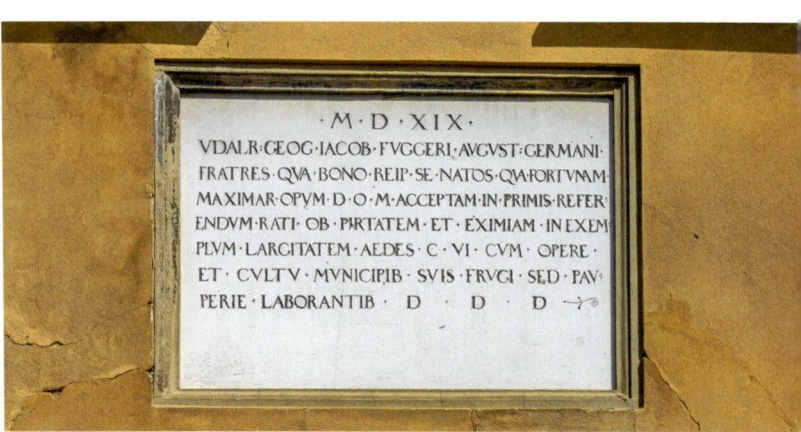

Often seen: the lily coat of arms

The coat of arms with the double lily was granted to the Fugger family by Emperor Friedrich III in 1473 and has been used ever since. It can be seen in several spots at the Fuggerei, for example in the form of heraldic stones above several entrances and portals. The coat of arms also appears frequently in Augsburg's townscape. Not only on existing or former Fugger houses, but also in many churches where the Fugger family were active as benefactors.

The coat of arms stones above the gates at Jakobsplatz and Sparrenlech certainly date from the time of Jakob Fugger; the stones at today's main gate from 1574 at the latest. After the destruction during the Second World War, they were salvaged from the ruins of the gate building and installed in the new building. In heraldry, the coat of arms, which in the case of the Fugger family shows a pair of lilies, is accompanied by the so-called heraldic helmet. The helmet of the Fugger coat of arms bears a lily between two buffalo horns (in color: blue-gold split) and has buffalo ears on the right and left.

A pretty corner: the Höchstetter oriel

When the new Senior Council Building was constructed, elements from destroyed Fugger houses and other historically significant buildings were also integrated. By doing so, they were preserved as so-called spolia. An example of this is the Höchstetter oriel. This masterpiece of Gothic stonemasonry dates back to 1507 and is thus older than the Fuggerei itself. Ambrosius Höchstetter, a merchant, banker and competitor of the Fugger family, had it made for his house on Kesselmarkt. The house was badly damaged during the Second World War, but the sandstone oriel was preserved. For a long time, there was no suitable place for the architectural jewel. It was not until 1962/63, when the Senior Council Building of the Fuggerei was extended, that a suitable environment was found. Beautiful details: the finely crafted coats of arms of the Höchstetter and Rehlinger families in the bottom row. Above are the coats of arms of the Habsburgs – an expression of Höchstetter's closeness to the imperial dynasty.

Höchstetter oriel after its destruction during the war and after its integration into the Senior Council Building of the Fuggerei.

ENTRANCE AREA

"I think it's nice that we are so well-known around the world. That so many people come here to see this social project."

Fuggerei resident

Doing good with your entrance fee

Approximately 220,000 people from all over the world visit the Fuggerei every year. This makes the social housing complex one of the most popular tourist attractions in Bavarian-Swabia. The entrance fee benefits the Fuggerei, for example for the maintenance of the flats. Since the revenue from forestry fluctuates greatly, that income is an important pillar for the foundation. Some Fuggerei residents are also working as cashiers at the ticket office, where they contribute to the community and earn some extra money. However, for them this is also about being in contact with others and the joy of knowing that the Fuggerei is an attractive destination.

IN THE MIDST OF LIFE

Markusplätzle

This secluded square was constructed when the enclosing buildings were erected after the Second World War. Today, Markusplätzle is a popular meeting place with a beer garden in the summer and a Christmas tree market in the Advent season.

In the winter, the Fuggerei has a special charm. The windows are decorated and show the Christmas story in Herrengasse. At Markusplätzle, the foresters of the Fugger Foundation and the construction team sell freshly cut, local Christmas trees for the benefit of the Fuggerei. For an all-round cozy outing, delicacies and mulled wine are offered in the midst of magical Christmas lights featuring a fire basket.

SAVING TIP

Every Christmas tree that is sold comes with a free annual ticket to the Fuggerei. One more reason for a winterly visit. Find the dates for the Christmas tree sale starting at the end of November at:
→ **www.fugger.de**

With time comes place

The Fuggerei model from 1909 clearly shows the difference between then and now. For a long time, there were only the alleyways with their intersections at the Fuggerei, but no squares like, for example, Markusplätzle. Instead, Herrengasse used to be separated from the adjacent property by a wall.

It is therefore assumed that originally the Fuggerei was less about community and more about the privacy of individual households. Additionally, the clear layout of the complex also promoted a certain control and discipline of the residents. At the end of the 19th century, an endowment from Prince Leopold Fugger-Babenhausen made it possible to purchase some adjacent properties to the west of the Fuggerei, including the Holeis estate vis-à-vis St. Mark's. This allowed the Fuggerei to be significantly expanded. Markusplätzle was built on these newly purchased premises after the Second World War.

Well-illustrated by the model (on the left): The wall on the upper part of Herrengasse closed off the Fuggerei grounds to the west at the level of the Holeis estate, where the administration of the Fuggerei was located after 1879. The Holeis estate was later transformed into Markusplätzle. To the right: A view of the Holeis estate from 1938.

The administration building

The administration building was destroyed in the Second World War and later rebuilt. The offices of the foundation's administration are located on the ground floor and the first floor. In the basement, the Leonhard's Chapel was rebuilt. The building is only accessible on certain occasions.

Gothic on the move: Leonhard's Chapel

Leonhard's Chapel formerly belonged to the Welser family on what is now Karolinenstraße. It was later converted into a restaurant and badly damaged during the Second World War. In agreement with the city of Augsburg and the Freyinger family, the last owners, the chapel found a new home in the administration building of the Fuggerei. The remaining parts were supplemented and reassembled

into an impressive vault with Gothic pointed arches. In 1966, by invitation of Joseph Ernst Prince Fugger von Glött, the Board of Trustees of the Swabian University consulted here, whose efforts led to inception of the University of Augsburg. Today, Leonhard's Chapel is still used for meetings and events.

Well hidden: the faun

Raimund von Doblhoff, the architect who rebuilt the Fuggerei, was an avid collector of architectural curiosities. He had some of them installed at the Fuggerei, such as the wine-wreathed faun's face. The horned creature probably once served as a gargoyle on a fountain.

House of the administrator

The administrator traditionally lives in an official residence on the Fuggerei grounds. In the past, this flat was situated in the gate building, today's Senior Council Building. At that time, the administrator collected the rent for the Fuggerei flats and supervised the residents. After the Second World War, a new house was built for the administrator at Markusplätzle. Today, the administrator acts as a manager for the Fugger Foundations.

Psalm board

The origin of this plaque next to the administrator's house is unclear. Nevertheless, Markusplätzle is ideal for a quiet reflection on the meaning of life with Psalm 90: "The years of our life are seventy, or even by reason of strength eighty; yet their span is but toil and trouble; they are soon gone, and we fly away."

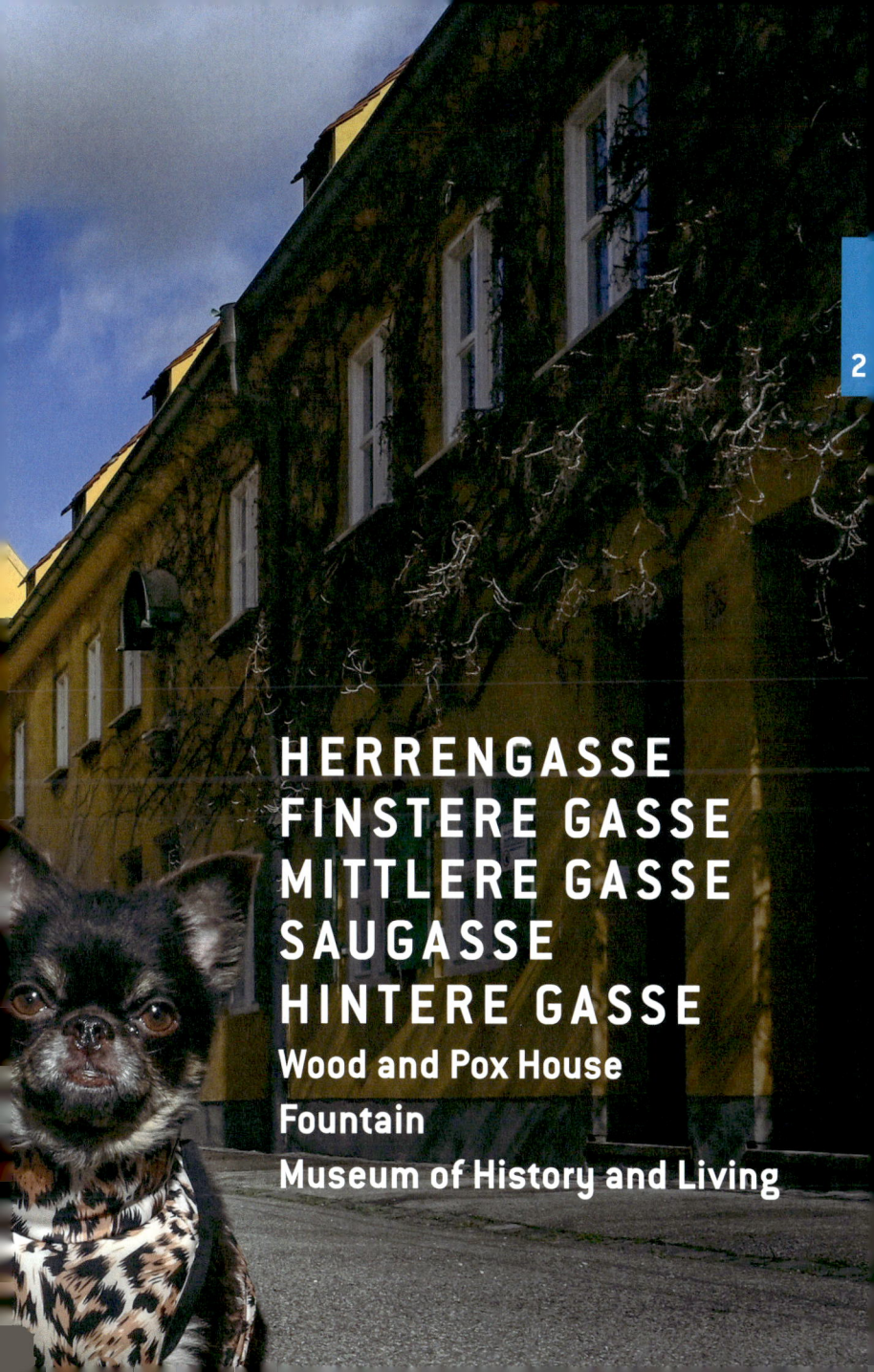

HERRENGASSE
FINSTERE GASSE
MITTLERE GASSE
SAUGASSE
HINTERE GASSE

Wood and Pox House

Fountain

Museum of History and Living

2

STRAIGHT AHEAD: HERRENGASSE

Home starts here

Already in the entrance area, the perfectly straight layout of the Fuggerei becomes apparent, with Herrengasse as the main axis, from which the other alleyways branch off to the right and left. However, this now central alley was built only after Saugasse located to the east. This can still be seen in the order of the Fuggerei house numbers, which began 500 years ago with the number 1 in Saugasse. Today, Herrengasse is the meeting point for all those who live or work in the Fuggerei or visit it. Since the early days of photography, it has been one of the most frequently captured motifs in the Fuggerei. It is also the ideal starting point through the Fuggerei of the residents – a warm welcome to their midst!

Well planned, well done

With the Fuggerei, Jakob Fugger and his master builder Thomas Krebs created an innovation whose details were extremely well thought out. From the very beginning, the complex was known for its functionality, quality and relatively high living comfort. In Herrengasse, several features catch the eye.

When the Fuggerei was built, it set new standards in terms of dimension and structure. Terraced houses were already known at the time – but an entire housing complex? That was new and remained remarkable even later on, as the poet Salomon Frenzel praised in 1585:

"See how many years ago they / made much lovelier streets than today / built in perfect rows / as if you were looking at a city / a grand row of beautiful homes / they set up one by one, brand new /"

Herrengasse

HEAVENLY

The sculpture at the corner of Markusplätzle and Herrengasse depicts the Archangel Michael defeating the devil with his sword. Seventeen such house saints and house Madonnas can be found in the Fuggerei. In the Gothic period, it was already common to put houses under the protection of a specific saint. When Augsburg became Protestant during the Reformation, many house saints disappeared from the facades. Especially during the Baroque period, Catholic believers could increasingly express their faith openly through house Madonnas again, and thus, Baroque Madonnas in particular adorn many old houses in the city center. Sculptures of saints, however, remained rare. But in the consistently Catholic-influenced Fuggerei, many house saints can be found, including some unique representations in Augsburg, such as St. Florian.

HOUSE MADONNAS AND HOUSE SAINTS

IN THE FUGGEREI

Figure	House No.	Figure	House No.
Mary medallion	3	Altötting figure of grace	38
St. Nepomuk	8	Christ in the Dungeon	41, 63
Mary and Child	16	St. Florian	51
St. Joseph and Child Jesus	17	St. Michael	57
Madonna with Halo	19	Angel figure	65
Madonna on a Crescent Moon	22	Our Lady of Sorrows	66
Mary relief	23		

OUTSIDE THE FUGGEREI

Risen Christ
Jakobsplatz, gate to Finstere Gasse — A1

Mary and Child
administrator's house, on garden side — A2

Two monks Sparrenlech 8 — A3

Two entrances for dignity

The terraced houses consist of a first-floor and an upper-floor unit. Instead of a shared staircase, each flat can be accessed separately from the street. This strengthened the awareness of having an own household and thus the sense of dignity of the residents. But the separate entrances also support a certain degree of social control: It is easy to monitor who enters and leaves which flat. Although, by their own accounts, the Fuggerei residents very much appreciate their direct access.

On the ground floor, the flat can be entered directly, while a staircase leads to the upper floor.

The typical Fuggerei flat

For 500 years, people have lived almost continuously in the Fuggerei. This is only possible because here, too, many things have evolved. For example, in the past, the flats didn't have a bathroom, but a kitchen, two chambers and a living room. The standard flat has always been around 60 square meters in size but today has two rooms, a kitchen and a bathroom. However, there are also one-room flats and others that are up to 140 square meters with three or four rooms for families. Traditionally, most ground-floor flats come with a small garden or courtyard. In return, the attic is assigned to the upper-floor flats as additional storage space. The flats meet today's standards; they have modern bathrooms, district heating, TV and internet. The individual furnishings are provided by the residents.

Even half is still valuable

In difficult times, flats were often shared so that more people could find a home in the Fuggerei. For example, after the Thirty Years' War, but also during industrialization or after the World Wars, two households often shared one flat. Even single rooms with shared use of kitchen and toilet were in demand during such times.

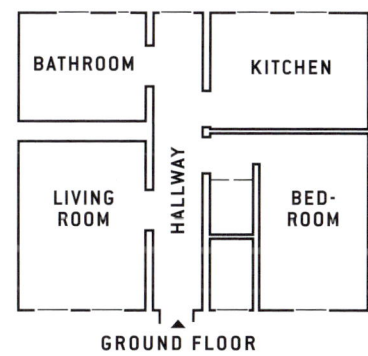

Designed for living and working

To this day, the spacious layout of the flats remains an important part of Jakob Fugger's idea of supporting fellow citizens in need. Because unlike in the typical almshouses back then, it was possible to work from home, and there was room for the whole family. Many craftsmen among the Fuggerei residents set up their workshops in the living room or a chamber, the attic, courtyard or in the wooden hut. This way, they saved money and could make a better living from their work's income. In the Fuggerei, weavers, dyers, butchers, cobblers, tailors and even a blacksmith could be found. The women often did home-based work as spinners, seamstresses or laundresses.

Even in the 1950s, some Fuggerei residents still worked as tailors or cobblers in their own homes.

HOUSING IS A PRIORITY

Except for a few buildings for administration, workshops and museums, all houses in the Fuggerei are reserved for residential purposes. Flats are only left vacant when larger renovations are planned, such as a new bathroom, after someone moves out. Residents often live in the Fuggerei for decades, so standards differ from place to place.

Experiencing community in the Fuggerei meeting place

The successful coexistence in the housing complex is supported by activities organized by the social workers of the Fuggerei, as well as by residents and external volunteers. At the center of this is the Fuggerei meeting place in house No. 57. Here, a wide range of community events take place, from the weekly breakfast and kaffeeklatsch to readings, concerts and movie nights.

"After more than 40 years of work, I was lucky enough to be offered a flat in the Fuggerei. Because I love the city of Augsburg, and the Fuggerei in particular. But today, I could no longer afford to live in the city. Here, I can engage in my gastronomic profession again through volunteer work, which makes me very happy."

Fuggerei resident

The "Widows' Buildings"

After the Second World War, two buildings were constructed in Herrengasse and Neue Gasse with single rooms, shared kitchen and toilet facilities for widows or widowers and single persons. Later, some of the rooms were combined again to create flats of different sizes.

Wilhelm Schmid

CAN "FEELING AT HOME" BE PLANNED?

What a homey atmosphere! Strolling through the Fuggerei is always a beautiful experience. Even back when I was a young man and spent ten formative years in Augsburg, I enjoyed doing that. Here, the world was whole, which helped me when my own world came apart. Later, during visits to my hometown, I showed my new Berlin-based family the gem that is the Fuggerei.

WILHELM SCHMID

born in 1953 in a district of Krumbach in Bavarian Swabia, lives as a freelance philosopher and author in Berlin. He studied philosophy and history in Berlin, Paris and Tübingen, and taught philosophy as an adjunct professor at the University of Erfurt. In 2021, his book "Heimat finden – Vom Leben in einer ungewissen Welt" (publ. by Suhrkamp) was published.

The Fuggerei is proof: Yes, feeling at home can be planned. All you need is experienced people with a good intuition, much like in cooking. What are the ingredients? A human measure. The buildings should not overwhelm residents and visitors with their sheer size, but promise them a sense of security, because that is what home is: familiarity and security. The rooms can radiate that before they are even entered. Corners, oriels, nooks create favorite spots and safe places from which the hustle and bustle of the world can be observed. Right next door, neighbors should live to avoid feeling lonely and forlorn, as can easily happen in anonymous, giant buildings. On the street where the buildings line up, people should feel safe, because home also means protection. Where insecurity prevails, security becomes impossible. Home provides certainty in a uncertain world. It's allowed to have an idyllic appearance. Idylls are peaceful. Everyone knows that life and the world are not purely idyllic, but everyone also loves spaces for retreat, here they are not constantly exposed to all kinds of dangers.

Home definitely needs a restaurant, a café, to be able to leave the familiar environments behind for a moment. How wonderful it is to relax in hospitable surroundings with a cup of coffee and perhaps chat with others – "ratschen", as it is called in Augsburg. For strangers, the restaurant is a way to get behind the facades instead of having to stop in front of them. How much this can be missed was painfully evident to everyone when restaurants were closed during the Corona pandemic of 2020/21.

So is that bourgeois? Yes, in the best sense! All societies depend on people who take pride in their surroundings. Who care about things. Such citizens enjoy living in a society that gives them space so that they can have a sense of belonging. In a society that pushes people physically to the margin and beyond, a sense of responsibility does not develop. The Fuggerei was and still is the successful attempt to build a home for those who would otherwise have been marginalized.

"Everyone knows that life and the world are not purely idyllic, but everyone also loves spaces for retreat, where they are not constantly exposed to all kinds of dangers."

Wilhelm Schmid

BEAUTY IN THE DETAILS

Nostalgic gas lanterns

In 1864, a – at that time – very modern street lighting system was installed in the Fuggerei: Nine gas lanterns now illuminated the compounds' alleyways. And even though electric light was introduced in the 20th century, six gas lanterns were preserved in the Fuggerei following a decision in 1976. Today, they are connected to the modern gas network of the municipal utilities and, as the last remaining gas lanterns in Augsburg, they also make eyes sparkle with their warm glow.

Individual bell pulls

Each of the wrought-iron handles on the doorbell pulls of the Fuggerei flats is slightly different from the others. Because for centuries, alleys and streets in the cities were not lit at night, but rather pitch-black. The different handles made it probably easier for the Fuggerei residents to find their way when returning home late. Even if the temptation is great, please do not pull the handles; most bell pulls work.

Biedermeier look

The warm ocher tone of the Fuggerei facades, the white window frames and the rich green of the window shutters only came into fashion, and into the Fuggerei, around the mid-19th century during the Biedermeier period. Before that, the facades were plastered in the grayish-yellow tone of Augsburg's mason sand. The wooden window shutters were probably natural in color.

Distinctive roofs

The stepped gables with their distinctive roof ornaments are typical of house construction in Augsburg at the time the Fuggerei was built. The dormers were also common during that time. Whereas the so-called Russian chimneys have only existed in the Fuggerei since the beginning of the 20th century. They gradually replaced the bigger German chimneys, because thanks to their smaller cross section, they have a better draft.

Shingle charm

Until the late 19th century, the roofs of the Fuggerei were still covered with a tile roofing made of "Haggen and Preiß" (also known as "Monk and Nun") and often covered in moss. The rain gutters had long, beak-like extensions supported by iron rods, over which the rainwater was directed into the alleys. Until the Fuggerei was fully connected to the sewer system, the water flowed through the alleys through open rain gutters.

SIDE TRIP TO FINSTERE GASSE

SECLUDED AND PEACEFUL

Finstere Gasse

Actually, Finstere Gasse ("Dark Alley") is rather bright. Perhaps the name refers to the shaded courtyards between Finstere and Mittlere Gasse. From the outside, these courtyards are not visible. On the north side of the alley, however, there are proper gardens – created by their owners and protected by walls. The gate at the end of the alley, like all Fuggerei gates, was open to pedestrians during the day until 2006.

View into the courtyards of Finstere Gasse

More light!

Originally, the window openings in the Fuggerei were smaller and in some cases not as many as today. But they were already made of bull's-eye glass instead of oiled linen or parchment, as was still common at that time. However, windows in the 16th century were made of greenish, so-called forest glass, much likely creating subdued lighting conditions. As larger windows became common and more affordable, the openings in the Fuggerei were also enlarged; mostly during renovations, for example, after the destruction caused by the Swedes during the Thirty Years' War.

READING TIP

In the small book "Barfuss durch die Finstere Gass" ("Barefoot through Finstere Gasse"), author Reiner Schmidt describes his childhood with his grandparents in the Fuggerei before and during the Second World War. His memoirs paint an authentic and touching picture of the time from a child's perspective.

Visiting the Holzwart family in the 16th century

The Holzwarts lived in the Fuggerei from 1520 until at least 1552, including at Finstere Gasse 28. Jörg Holzwart worked as a wood measurer, his wife Afra was a housewife. They had three children. Jörg's work began at dawn and ended at nightfall – so in the summer, his workday was longer than in the winter. As a wood measurer, Jörg was out and about a lot. When the loggers delivered their firewood to the city, Jörg verified the stated delivery quantity with the customers. For this purpose, he had to stack the wood to a specific width and height. His work was exhausting and poorly paid. After work, he had dinner with his family. They sat in the living room, which could also be heated if necessary. Small oil lamps provided some light. But oil and tallow for lighting cost money and were used sparingly. It was therefore common to go to sleep shortly after nightfall.

NIGHT LIGHT

In the chambers of the Fuggerei flats, a niche provided a safe place to put oil lamps or pine chips. Pine chips were affordable but burned only for a short time. The resinous pieces of wood were placed in a holder and lit. They gave enough light to orient oneself for a few minutes – for example, to undress and go to bed.

Jörg Holzwart with measuring stick. (Fictional depiction)

AT THE CROSSROADS

For cures against syphilis: the Wood and Pox House

At the end of the 15th century, the "French disease" or "smallpox", now known as syphilis, began to spread in Europe. Treatments with mercury or the wood of the subtropical guaiac tree were regarded as a remedy. As early as 1520, still during Jakob Fugger's lifetime, such "wood treatments" were also administered in the Fuggerei. Poor people suffering from syphilis or similar symptoms could receive a wood treatment over the course of several weeks, which included mainly decoctions from guaiac wood, along with smoke applications, sweat baths and bloodletting, all free of charge. For the treatments, the three houses No. 40 to 42 were combined into what was called the Wood and Pox House. The famous Augsburg physician Adolph Occo II and his successors provided medical guidance. The funding was initially covered by private funds of the Fuggers; from 1548 onwards, it was provided by the Wood and Pox House Foundation of Anton Fugger and his nephews. The up to 22 patients were only required to make a confession as their contribution. And did it work? Medical records in the Fugger Archives describe successful cures as well as treatment failures. In the mid-17th century, the doors of the Wood and Pox House were closed for good. But the Wood and Pox House Foundation still exists and funds the maintenance of the three houses No. 40 to 42.

FUGGER AND GUAIAC

Guaiac wood was imported through ports in Antwerp, Lisbon and Seville and distributed through pharmacies. However, the physicians in the Fuggerei obtained it directly from the Fugger's trading posts in the port cities. Proponents of the competing mercury treatment accused the Fuggers of enriching themselves through the sale of guaiac wood. The numbers, however, show that the profit margin was very low and the trade with guaiac wood had only a small share in the Fugger's business volume. Their trade network could easily obtain the guaiac wood.

Picturesque fountain

As a popular postcard motif even more than a century ago, the fountain scenery conveyed an idyllic image of the settlement to the world– although especially drawing water was hard work, of course. Nonetheless: At the fountain, people could always have a little chat, a "Ratsch". Well into the 20th century, people filled their buckets here until finally, in the course of reconstruction after the Second World War, running water became available in the flats.

No one draws water here anymore, but the fountain still is a beautiful sight.

History of the fountain

Already in the 16th century, the Fuggerei was equipped with water wells, which were probably supplied by a private well system and later by municipal water towers. By 1635, there were already three tube wells in operation in the Fuggerei, providing drinking and domestic water. Special feature: The water from such tube wells could be drawn with "elegant" ease, instead of having to use muscle power to pump it out of the ground. An earlier version of the fountain in Herrengasse probably existed as early as 1599: a wooden tube well, which was used until 1744, when it was replaced by a stone well. Since 1846, a cast-iron bowl fountain is splashing in its place.

The bench by the fountain is the traditional spot for Fuggerei residents to meet from time to time and exchange news about the world and the Fuggerei.

THROUGH MITTLERE GASSE

Also here: the Mozarts

Direct ancestors of the famous Wolfgang Amadeus Mozart lived in house No. 14 on Mittlere Gasse: his great-grandparents Franz and Anna. Franz Mozart (born October 3, 1649) became a master bricklayer like his father and brother. Because the brothers Mozart had carried the coffin at the funeral of an assistant executioner in 1677 – which was considered dishonorable at the time because of the deceased's profession – they were almost banned from their trade.

On the plaque, the year of death of Wolfgang Amadeus' great-grandfather Franz is stated incorrectly. Franz Mozart actually died in 1694.

> **UNCLEAR CIRCUMSTANCES**
>
> Whether Franz Mozart worked in the Fuggerei as a builder for the foundation, as is sometimes claimed, cannot be proven. Certainly, he pursued some kind of work, but entries in the tax records show that in the last five years of his life he could barely afford to pay the head tax and the "night guard's fee" ("Wachgeld"). The low tax rate indicates financial difficulties. It's possible that he suffered from an illness or had a frail constitution, so that he could not work much and therefore had to move to the Fuggerei. To this day, the reasons remain in the dark.

However, in the end, the scandal had no consequences. In 1678, Franz married Anna Härrer, who came from a poor family of day laborers. In 1681, they moved to the Fuggerei. With their three children, they lived at Mittlere Gasse 14, where Franz Mozart died at the young age of 45. As was usual at the time, the widow and her children had to move into so-called widows' quarters in house No. 22. Franz and Anna's eldest son Johann Georg later began an apprenticeship to become a master bookbinder. His son Leopold Mozart became known as a composer and musician – as well as the father and tireless supporter of Wolfgang Amadeus.

Timeless art: the compass maker Schrettegger

He was the last exponent of a great Augsburg crafts tradition: Johann Nepomuk Schrettegger, compass and sundial maker (born around 1765). He created numerous timepieces that are now displayed in museums around the world. Unfortunately, Schrettegger's exceptional skills came a little too late – with the onset of the industrialization, the handicraft production of clocks was no longer profitable. In 1818, he requested admission to the Fuggerei because of his "miserable financial situation due to the complete collapse of his business". In 1823, the family moved to Mittlere Gasse 18. In the Fuggerei, Schrettegger continued to pursue his craft until he passed away in 1843.

The elaborate timepieces created by Johann Nepomuk Schrettegger are now on display in museums worldwide.

VISIBLE GRADIENT

The Jakobervorstadt quarter is situated lower than the "Oberstadt" ("upper town") featuring town hall and Perlach tower. The view from Mittlere Gasse is scenic. But it also highlights the social difference between the splendidly constructed upper town of the Renaissance period and the quarter on the then-outskirts of the city, where mainly poor day laborers and small craftsmen lived.

MUSEUM OF HISTORY AND LIVING

Start of the exhibition: house No. 14
For half a millennium, the Fuggerei has been fulfilling the foundation's mission. The theme of this exhibition is the great ideas, events and decisions during this long period, as well as the relevant individuals from Jakob Fugger to the present day. Pictures, graphics and texts convey the most important information. In-depth insights are provided by interactive stations with exciting animations, audio and video contributions.

Room 1: How it all began
What were the reasons for the foundation of the Fuggerei in 1521? What was the cosmopolitan city of Augsburg like back then, why could the Fugger family rise here in particular, what were the social conditions like? Room 1 provides interesting facts about life in Augsburg, the Fugger family and Jakob Fugger's motivation as a founder.

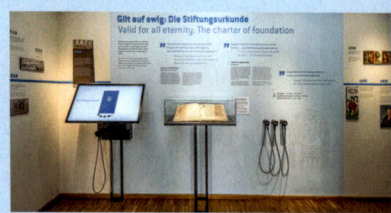

Room 2: Valid forever – the charter of foundation
One guilder (today 88 cents) annual rent, three prayers a day, needy Augsburgers of the Catholic faith: Why do these and other stipulations apply in the Fuggerei? They are laid down in the charter of foundation of 1521, as are other innovative and far-sighted provisions. The original document is on display as a facsimile; a media station explains its interpretation over time and why its core ideas apply eternally. Including a guessing game on the guilder, films on the funding of the Fuggerei and an audio version of the three prayers.

Room 2-3: The course of history

The most important milestones of the Fuggerei in their historical context: A timeline shows the development – from the social situation in Augsburg in 1475 to the reconstruction of the Fuggerei after the Second World War. Also: the A-Z of the Fugger Foundations in a digital encyclopedia.

Room 3:
Foundations – a family affair

The Fuggerei is meant to exist forever, as are the other eight Fugger Foundations. How Jakob Fugger's successors have fulfilled this mission in spite of many crises over the last 500 years and what ideas exist for the future of the Fuggerei are the subjects explored here. With interactive graphics and short animated films on the key individuals, events and decisions.

Passage to Mittlere Gasse 13: "Living Space" Fuggerei

People, stories and structures from 500 years take center stage in this room. In detailed animated videos, life in the Fuggerei is illuminated, from architecture and historical events to the touching fates of some of the residents.

Inside the historical original: house No. 13

Parts of the exhibition rooms in this house date back as far as 1517. The furnishings have been reconstructed according to historical designs. However, the Fuggerei residents could always furnish their homes completely individually. What their everyday life might have been like in the different rooms and eras is depicted by captivating visualizations and audio stories. For this purpose, biographies of residents from five centuries were researched in the Fugger Archives and the Augsburg City Archives.

A walk through 500 years: the corridor

Here, the stories on living in the Fuggerei begin – stories of and with five families, historically documented as Fuggerei residents. Ceiling and walls of the corridor are made of wooden boards, as in the time of the Fuggerei's construction. Here's also the entrance to one of the toilets that became common in the housing complex after 1890. After the Second World War, the connection to the city's sewer system allowed for the installation of flush toilets.

Good housekeeping: the kitchen

At the time when the Fuggerei was built, the kitchen was used only for cooking and heating; only later did it serve as dining place. Also, personal hygiene was practiced in the kitchen, where water could be heated. How the kitchen worked, which furniture, utensils and food were used by the families, are not only shown through reconstructed objects, but also through two media stations with impressive stories and pictures spanning five centuries.

All-purpose room: the living room

In the shifting use of rooms, historical change becomes evident: Historically, the heated living room used to be a place to work, eat and spend time with the family. It was not until the end of the 19th century that it started to serve as the "best room" or the "front room", the precursor to our modern living room. At the media stations, digital time travels offer vivid insights into the various uses of the rooms, living conditions and working worlds of the historic Fuggerei families.

Come to rest: the bedroom

With two unheated chambers, a Fuggerei flat offered a relatively large amount of space for flexible use. This allowed, for example, families to arrange enough sleeping places. Also, the flats could be divided relatively easily, for example, into two widow households. How the furnishings changed over time is a topic covered by the media station. Another topic is the worries and thoughts that kept residents awake at night. They are presented in fictional interviews, based on documents from the Fugger Archives and other historical sources.

DETAILS OF THE FLATS

USEFUL, FUNCTIONAL, GOOD.

The Fuggerei's architecture has a unique charm, but it also impresses with functional ideas. The interior, too, was equipped with useful details that increased comfort and safety. To this day, some of them still stand the test of time.

Build flexibly, cook safely

In the past, the interior walls of the Fuggerei flats were made of wooden boards plastered with layers of clay and straw. Fabrication of these non-load-bearing walls was inexpensive, and they could be easily relocated. The kitchens, on the other hand, were constructed with a stone vault. The solid masonry reduced the risk of fire, and the vault shape kept the heat in the room. Also later, stoves – from wood-burning to electric – were part of the basic equipment of the flats.

See through and pass through

The small window between living room and kitchen provides ventilation and can also be found in other houses from the time of the Fuggerei's construction. But it also helps to keep an eye on what's going on in the living room from the kitchen. Furthermore, it served as a small pass-through.

Clean heating

Fuggerei flats are generally not furnished but have always been equipped with a heating option. In the beginning, there were built-in tiled stoves in the living rooms, which were later replaced by cast-iron stoves. They were heated from the kitchen, through a stove door next to the kitchen stove. This kept smoke and dirt in the kitchen. Today, the Fuggerei is supplied with sustainable district heating by the municipal utilities. It is generated, among other sources, in a biomass combined heat and power plant that also utilizes wood waste from the foundation's forests.

Open conveniently

With a door opener in the wall leading to the corridor, the front door cold be opened without leaving the warm living room. This saved heating costs and was also very convenient. However, the door openers were not installed before the 17th or 18th century.

Store smartly

Beneath a trap door in the corridor, a small pantry is hidden. Due to the high groundwater level, the Fuggerei could not be equipped with a basement – but at least this provided a small, cool storage space in the past.

IN THE FUGGEREI'S OLDEST ALLEY

A lively history

The first houses of the Fuggerei were not built on Herrengasse, which nowadays is very central, but rather further east on Saugasse ("Pig Alley"). The alley got its name because of its proximity to the former Saumarkt ("Pig Market"), where the Augsburg pig market had been held since 1438. After its closure, the name was changed to the more dignified Jakobsplatz ("Jacob's Square") in 1877. The public fountain on the square was also improved. Since 1888, the Neptune Fountain has been splashing here displaying a bronze figure of the Roman sea god with his attribute, the trident.

Stone guardian

The gate between Saugasse and Jakobsplatz is guarded by a "mascaron" on the inside. Such stone faces were placed as ornaments on facades and above gateways especially in the Renaissance and again in the 19th century – but certainly not in the original Fuggerei. The mascaron is probably a found object that architect Doblhoff integrated to add a little touch during the reconstruction of the Fuggerei after the Second World War.

Useful: the infirmary

With the founding of the Fuggerei, house No. 1 on Saugasse was designated as the infirmary for Fugger servants. A general hospital with six beds and year-round service was established in 1523 with the construction of house No. 52 on Ochsengasse. Around 1650 it was closed down like the "Wood and Pox House". Also later on, medical or nursing care was provided temporarily on site, and in some cases, special rooms were set up for this purpose.

Clever: the world's first house numbers

Cities with tens of thousands of inhabitants, but without clear addresses: In the Augsburg tax records of 1519, the residents of the Fuggerei are already listed with their house numbers. Elsewhere, people continued to make do with long-winded and vague descriptions, often based on house names or close-by prominent landmarks such as a gate, a church or a market. It was not until 1708 that house numbers were used in London, a little later in Paris and Prague. In the rest of Augsburg, house numbers were not introduced until 1781.

Gothic numbers 4 and 17

Gothic beauty

The digits of the house numbers were hand-carved into bricks – at that time still using Gothic numbers, recognizable by the "half" 8 instead of a 4. Which of today's house numbers are original or replicas remains unclear.

Let it flow (off)!

At least since the mid-16th century, the Lauterlech (a canalized arm of the river "Lech") was led into the Fuggerei, flowing openly through Saugasse and a section of Hintere Gasse and then leaving the Fuggerei walls. In addition to drainage during rainfall, the Lauterlech was used for waste disposal and as a toilet. From 1890 onwards, lavatories with buckets were installed in the Fuggerei flats for this purpose. In 1909, planning began for the connection to the sewer system. The Lauterlech was covered.

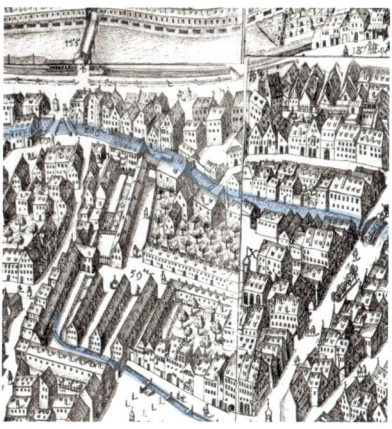

The Fuggerei on the so-called "Kilianplan" from 1626

GARDEN BLISS

In the gardens and courtyards of the ground-floor flats, there is much beauty blooming in secret; yet some paradises can be admired as one passes by, such as in Hintere Gasse. In the past, residents used their outdoor spaces for work, wood storage, growing potatoes, vegetables and fruit, or for keeping small livestock. In 1816, resident Christina Heichele of Hintere Gasse 11, was even allowed to build a stable and keep a cow. Instead of "moo", today, there's birdsong and the occasional "meow" or "woof" – which is also nice.

Prof. Dr. Dietmar Schiersner, Fugger-Archives

WHAT IS SPECIAL ABOUT JAKOB FUGGER'S MOTIVATION?

PROF. DR. DIETMAR SCHIERSNER

is a professor for "History of the Middle Ages and the Early Modern Age and its Didactics" at the University of Education Weingarten since 2006, since 2014 also scientific director of the "Fürstlich und Gräflich Fuggersches Familien- und Stiftungsarchiv" (the Fugger Archives).

In a society characterized by ethical concepts such as gratitude, solidarity or honor, donations and foundations create or strengthen social bonds – among contemporary fellow citizens, but also with regard to posterity ("Memoria").

Characteristic of the culture of the late Middle Ages is also the religious horizon: the sanctioning of giving as a commandment of Christian charity and its transcendental connection to the personal hope of salvation. The Fuggerei foundation is based on these premises: It's an expression of gratitude from the founders to the community that enabled the economic and social success of the Fugger family; it corresponds to the Christian commandment of Caritas; and it anticipates a hereafter in which the good deed will be rewarded. Also, the grateful thoughts and intercessory prayers of the beneficiaries continuously contribute to the salvation of the founders and their families.

But the Fuggerei foundation goes beyond what was customary until then, not only because of the size of the foundation's capital and the immense number of

beneficiaries: With the Fuggerei, something new is realized – for a clientele that is mostly still able to work, and with unprecedented architectural consistency, an early modern concept of helping people to help themselves is realized, which today would be referred to as "empowerment". The residents are not primarily serving as cogs in a late medieval "prayer machine". Instead, earning one's own living, which is both intended and structurally encouraged in and by the settlement, assumes central importance: In fact, although nowhere made explicit, the founders Jakob Fugger and his brothers attributed prayer-like effects to it.

Considering the innovative nature of the Fuggerei, it becomes clear that the effects of the Memoria, both on this side and on the other, cannot entirely explain Jakob Fugger's approach to foundations. After all, for this purpose, he could have simply adopted and exceeded the existing models. Very likely, there was something else, too, that also motivates founders today: Along with social and religious purposes, the desire for creative expression is realized, a desire to conceive something unique and – thanks to the resources available – bring it into reality. In this sense, the Fuggerei is, quite literally, the "creation" of Jakob Fugger.

> "With the Fuggerei, something new is realized – for a clientele that is mostly still able to work, and with unprecedented architectural consistency, an early modern concept of helping people to help themselves is realized, which today would be referred to as "empowerment"."
>
> Dietmar Schiersner

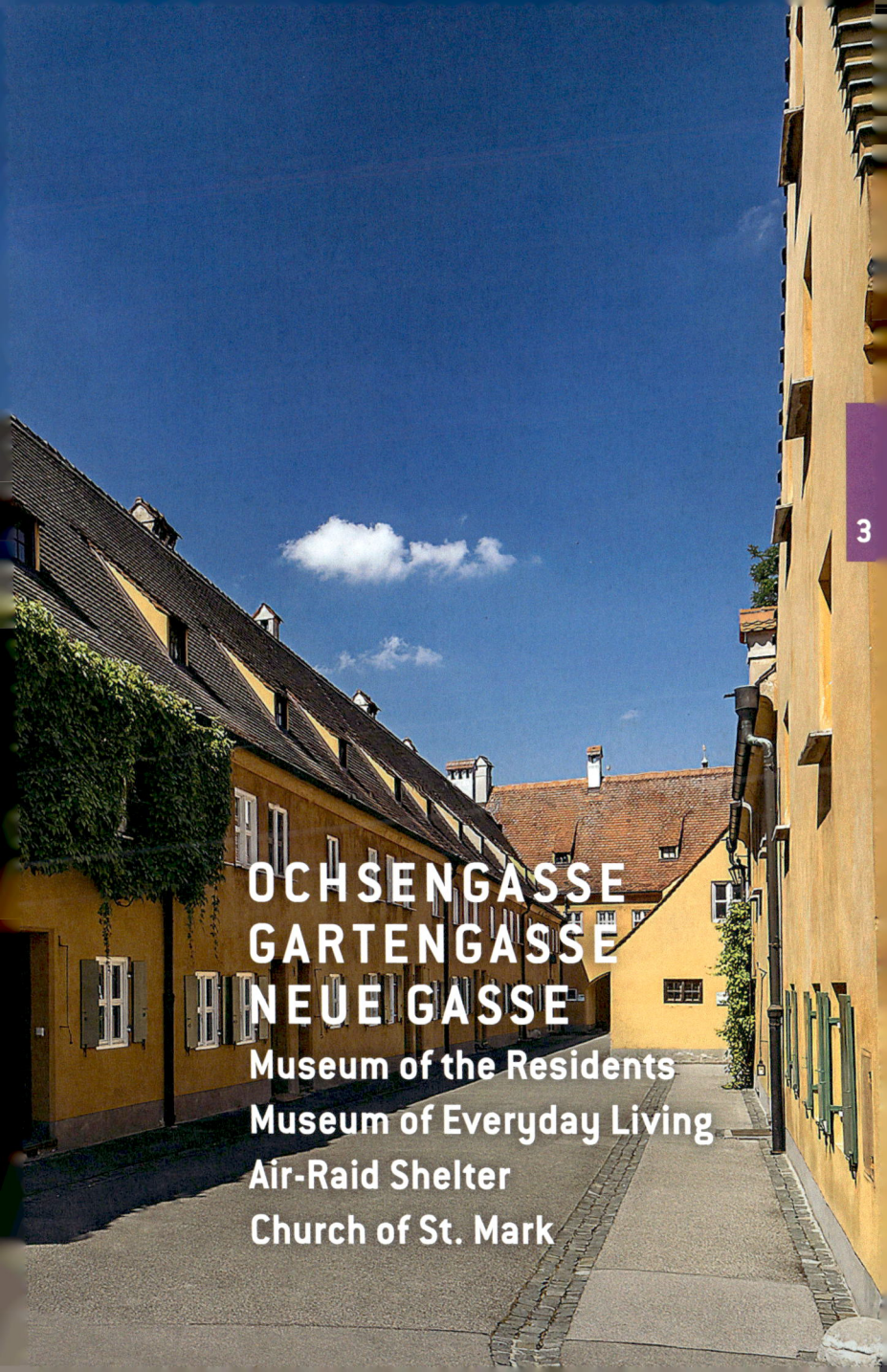

OCHSENGASSE
GARTENGASSE
NEUE GASSE

Museum of the Residents
Museum of Everyday Living
Air-Raid Shelter
Church of St. Mark

3

IN THE YOUNGEST PART OF THE FUGGEREI

Expansion after the Second World War

The Jakobervorstadt was heavily damaged by air raids during the Second World War. Not only the Fuggerei lay in ruins; the neighboring houses and streets were also devastated. This situation provided an opportunity to significantly expand the Fuggerei after the war. Several ruined properties next to the Fuggerei could be acquired through foundation funds. As a result of the expansion, the Fuggerei now covers a total area of 18,000 square meters.

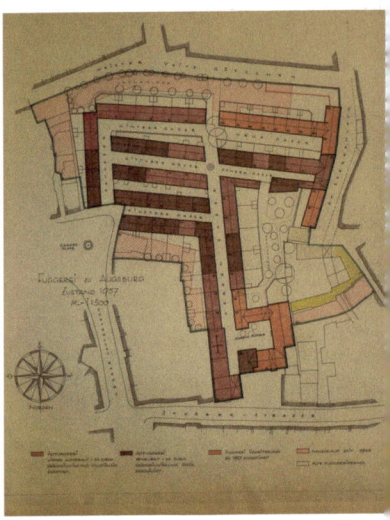

The most recent part of the Fuggerei today includes the park area along Meister-Veits-Gässchen and Gartengasse as well as Neue Gasse and the new buildings in the park near the air-raid shelter. Also, the gardens on both sides of Herrengasse were enlarged. This created room for new construction – twelve new houses and two so-called widows' buildings with one-room flats were built over time.

The name says it all

To this day, all you need to specify the address is: Fuggerei plus house number. Adding the name of the alley is really just a handy addition for the mailman. Nevertheless, as is often the case, the names of the alleys tell us something about their historical context: At the square in front of Saugasse (Pig Alley), the pig market was located for a long time, in front of Ochsengasse (Ox Alley), a cattle market. Herrengasse (Master Alley) refers to the administration building of "the master", Finstere (Dark), Mittlere (Middle) and Hintere (Rear) Gasse are self-explanatory. In old photos of the Fuggerei, you can still see the alley names on metal signs. In 1938, they were replaced with etched stone plaques. This noble signage was also used for the two alleyways that were created in the course of the expansion.

This photo from 1929 shows the square by the fountain before the expansion. Gartengasse and the extension of Neue Gasse do not yet exist.

OCHSENGASSE 46

THE MUSEUM OF THE RESIDENTS IN THE FUGGEREI

The "Museum of the Residents" is the authentic source for everything worth knowing about life in the Fuggerei today: Visitors learn who lives in the Fuggerei today and how to get a place there, what sets life here in this unique community apart from other places, and how the stipulations of the charter of foundation are implemented today. The multimedia exhibition in the four rooms of a Fuggerei flat provides interesting insights into the "cosmos" of the Fuggerei. At the media stations, residents themselves also have their say and share stories about life in the settlement.

Heart chamber

Fourteen residents of the Fuggerei bring the room to life with their personalities. They all contributed an object to the exhibition that is connected to their life in the Fuggerei. In short film clips, they share their thoughts and stories about these objects.

Movie room

Sit back and enjoy: Stories about the foundation and life in the Fuggerei.

"I am glad that I am here because my pension is small. It's really nice here. I just feel safe here, and it's so quiet! The many people who come to visit don't bother me at all. I sit in the back, I look out into my garden, and when the weather is fine, I sit outside on the bench in the garden. Otherwise, I'm usually in my kitchen reading. That's the way it is."

Fuggerei resident

Confidentiality room

What is the "secret" of the Fuggerei – why has Jakob Fugger's visionary legacy been functioning for more than 500 years? Here, answers are provided: from the unique structure and organization of the Fuggerei to the people responsible for its continued existence. This includes, for example, explaining the role of the Fugger family in the foundations as well as the responsibilities of the administration and the application process for a Fuggerei flat.

Living Space

An intense encounter with the core idea of the Fuggerei: While the housing complex is also a historical landmark and tourist magnet, it is first and foremost a home for about 150 people. Many of them show their faces here, and some answer the most frequently asked questions about life in the Fuggerei in short films. Also, typical misunderstandings and prejudices are addressed.

THE MUSEUM OF EVERYDAY LIFE IN THE FUGGEREI

Life and living in the Fuggerei have changed over the past 70 years – and so have the social conditions. From the bitter hardships of the post-war years to today's neediness: The Fuggerei fulfills its intended purpose – always with the means and ideas and to the standards of the time. The "Museum of Everyday Life" in a typical 60 square meter Fuggerei flat sheds light on this development through interesting historical objects.

Living room

From the post-war years to the present day, furnishings and how the rooms are used have changed significantly, as demonstrated by objects, films and images from the years of reconstruction. And what is life like in the Fuggerei today? This is shown by residents who have opened their doors to a cinematic tour of their homes and gardens.

"Many people think it's a museum, but that's not what we are here. We live in our regular flats here, like anyone else would in Augsburg. It's just a tad special and that people can visit us."

Fuggerei resident

Sleeping room

Different times, similar worries: Even though economic conditions were tougher in the past, in essence, everyday problems and fears are the same today. This is confirmed by records in the Fugger Archives and by the experiences of the social workers in the Fuggerei today. For the exhibition in this room, some examples have been juxtaposed.

Kitchen

Between table and cooking stove, everyday life has probably changed the most noticeably over the last 70 years. Managing the household without electrical appliances? That was hard work that took a lot of time. Also access to food and daily hygiene was much less convenient. Old objects from the Fuggerei, pictures and documents highlight the differences.

Bathroom

How living standard and comfort have continued to evolve in the Fuggerei as well is exemplified by the original bathroom of one resident. Starting in the 1970s, bathrooms were installed in all Fuggerei flats. Before that, there were usually only sinks and toilets; the residents bathed in the Fuggerei bathhouse or in the Municipal Bath.

A STORY BEHIND EVERY DOOR

Several thousand people have lived in the Fuggerei since its inception. Some of them have left biographical traces in the records of the Fugger Archives and in the Augsburg City Archives, which also reveal a lot about the respective circumstances of the time. Sometimes, the entire life story and fate of a resident can be reconstructed. Some of them are remembered in the museums and in the alleys of the Fuggerei – for example, on Ochsengasse.

Stolperstein (memorial stone) for Aloisia Kempter

A memorial stone in front of house No. 49 on Ochsengasse commemorates Aloisia Kempter, who was murdered in a killing center under the Nazi regime. Aloisia was born on August 23, 1890, and lived in the Fuggerei with her parents from 1913 onwards. Due to a cognitive disability, she required extensive care, which was a challenge for her parents, Alban and Christina Kempter. In 1934, Aloisia's mother died. Alban Kempter, an alcoholic, was overwhelmed by the care for his daughter, who was now in her forties, and the two moved out the same year. Aloisia lived in a municipal nursing home for a few months and was then transferred to "Schloss Lautrach", where she lived for the following years. Her father died in 1938. In 1941, Aloisia was taken to the district sanatorium and nursing home in Kaufbeuren-Irsee. Shortly thereafter, as part of the Nazi "Aktion T4" program, she was deported to the killing center "Schloss Hartheim" near Linz where she was murdered on August 8, 1941.

Dorothea Braun: Victim of the witch craze

The nurse Dorothea Braun, who lived with her husband, the "Vogelheuslmacher" (birdcage maker) Paulus Braun, at Ochsengasse 52 from 1615 on, gained sad notoriety. The Brauns had a son and two daughters. Their daughter Maria was to learn sewing from her aunt Apollonia, which led to a drama with a deadly ending, because conflicts between Apollonia and Dorothea escalated in the mutual accusation of being witches. Apollonia and her niece were imprisoned, with eleven-year-old Maria initially confirming the accusations against Apollonia during interrogation, but later accusing her own mother. Under torture, Dorothea Braun confessed to everything the councilors wanted to hear. In autumn 1625, she was convicted, executed by the sword and then burned – the first of 16 women in Augsburg to fall victim to the witch craze.

ALL-ROUND PROTECTION

Built for security

The wall around the Fuggerei was part of the complex from the very beginning, a quite common feature at that time. Many larger estates in the city had protective walls and were accessible only through gates that could be closed at any time. What is special is that in the Fuggerei, it has remained that way ever since. Although, after the destruction during the Second World War, there were considerations to remove the already damaged walls; in the end, the decision was made to rebuild them according to the historical design. Even today, the gates are closed at night. Then, only people who live or work in the Fuggerei are allowed to enter through the gate on Ochsengasse. Most of the Fuggerei residents are glad about this. For them, the wall does not mean a "gated community" type of separation, but rather peace, security and protection.

THE ACCESS CONCEPT

In the daytime, the gate on Jakoberstraße is open to everyone. With their keys, residents can also use other entrances. After 10 p.m., they enter through the gate on Ochsengasse.

Small contribution from the night owls. In addition to their salary from the foundation, the night guards also receive a small contribution from the residents to whom they open the gate at night: 50 cents before midnight and 1 euro afterwards.

At night, only through the Ochsentor (Ox Gate)

For a long time, the gate at Saugasse served as the night entrance and exit of the Fuggerei. Responsible for opening it was a gatekeeper from among the residents of the Fuggerei who was paid by the foundation. Today, the night entrance is located at the Ochsentor. However, the tradition still stands that residents of the Fuggerei can earn some extra money by serving as night guards and opening the entrance when needed. Currently, three night guards take turns providing this service. Every day at 10 p.m., the night guard on duty must lock the gates and unlock them again early in the morning at 4:30. In between, he or she stays in the night guard's room right by the gate and opens it for returning or departing residents.

Open eyes and ears

There are different strategies for enduring the demanding night watch. Some read books or solve crossword puzzles, while others watch television or take a short rest. In any case, when the doorbell rings, they have to be ready. Via a monitor and an intercom system, it is possible to check who is requesting entry.

Bright delight

Night watch duty also includes turning on the alley lights in the evening and turning them off again in the morning. In the 1950s, night guard Michael Burger often carried a picturesque lantern in his hand – much to the delight of the tourists.

Professor Dr. Kerstin Schlögl-Flierl

IS HELP DEVALUATED BY REQUESTING A SERVICE IN RETURN?

Response from an ethical and theological perspective

PROFESSOR DR. KERSTIN SCHLÖGL-FLIERL

holds the Chair of Moral Theology (Theological Ethics) at the Faculty of Catholic Theology at the University of Augsburg. Her research focuses include bioethics and ethics of relationships. Since May 2020, she is one of 26 members of the German Ethics Council.

Does help cease to be help – especially in the context of Christian charity – when reciprocation is demanded? Is the reciprocation a reasonable contribution or a profit-oriented transaction? Posing the question in this way focuses on the interaction between two individuals as a form of exchange. The question concerns the justice and proportionality of what transpires between two service providers. Is it just that the "rich" Fuggers expect reciprocation from the "less affluent" residents? Especially since prayers are included in the exchange.

But the question could also be approached from a different angle, namely from a care-ethical perspective. In such an approach, the question of what transpires between two people can no longer be understood merely as an exchange of goods between two essentially anonymous service providers. At the center of a care ethics approach is the question of care

(care-for, care-about, after-care) of people for each other, especially where asymmetrical relationships are involved (e.g., in a nursing home). It concerns the relationship between individuals who, by virtue of their humanity as such, are beings with various dimensions of neediness.

From a care-ethical perspective, reciprocation can be seen as the foundation of a relationship. This way, the Fuggerei does not become a 'soulless' institution; instead, the monetary and spiritual reciprocity creates the chance to bring more symmetry, more mutuality to asymmetrical relationships. Those who receive help become helpers on a different level. Perhaps, also a sense of gratitude arises in the giver, for the opportunity to live in the Fuggerei. So, it's not about monetary value but rather the value of relationships, which, in the Christian understanding, always surpasses material wealth.

Undoubtedly, demanding a prayer as reciprocation raises theological concerns. One can only adequately understand such a demand in the context of the piety and religious practices of that time. And today? A prayer is an intimate dialogue between God and man or woman ... expressing gratitude, requesting, pleading, lamenting. Moreover, demanding spiritual reciprocation in spiritually and religiously less harmonious times is unlikely to foster this relationship of God and man or woman. However, the basic insight of care ethics, to perceive humans as partially dependent, relational beings, is also of help here. Because even in their relationship to the divine, no one is alone on their journey. Rather, it is precisely through their neighbor that he or she finds their way to God, and to God never without their neighbor. Prayer as an expression of encouragement for and with one another traditionally holds an essential place in this context.

> "Because even in their relationship to the divine, no one is alone on their journey. Rather, it is precisely through their neighbor that he or she finds their way to God, and to God never without their neighbor."
>
> Kerstin Schlögl-Flierl

The carpentry: craft and heart

Since the post-war years, a Fuggerei construction unit has been taking care of all craftsman work in the settlement. The base and workshop of the construction teams is the carpentry on Ochsengasse. Here, for example, window shutters and doors are repaired or crafted. Due to the different states of construction – from the 16th century to today – the maintenance of the heritage-protected houses requires experience and a good instinct. The Fuggerei's craftsmen know every corner as well as the history and structure of all buildings in the Fuggerei, allowing them to carry out even tricky modernizations professionally, while saving time and costs.

In the early 17th century, there was a stable where the carpentry is located today.

Hard work: the reconstruction of the Fuggerei after the war

The tradition of keeping a Fuggerei construction unit dates back to the time of reconstruction after the war. Many of the construction workers and craftsmen in the Fuggerei were refugees at the time, who could temporarily reside there in makeshift accommodations due to the extreme housing shortage. Lockers in the attic of the carpentry still bear witness to this. The wood for the reconstruction came from the foundation's forests. Because building materials were in short supply everywhere, wood was also used as a means of exchange – for example, for cement.

New in the proven way

The houses along the Sparrenlech were built during the expansion of the complex. They integrate harmoniously into the architectural ensemble. The Senior Council placed a strong emphasis on high-quality architecture during the reconstruction, adhering to the historical dimensions and ensuring excellent craftsmanship. But this was also criticized: In 1947, the municipal building director praised the "truly astonishing high level of historicizing architectural features", but also questioned such an expense in these difficult times. However, since the reconstruction of the Fuggerei was financed solely from the foundation's assets, it remained as such: The destroyed Fuggerei regained its historical appearance. A fortunate circumstance until today.

Remembering Jakob Fugger

The bronze bust of Jakob Fugger has been placed here in the Fuggerei in 2007. It is a cast of an early-modern plaster bust in the Valhalla and Augsburg's only monument to the city's most famous founder. For several decades, Jakob Fugger has played a significant role in shaping Augsburg and European history, which is sometimes viewed controversially today. In any case, for centuries, his foundations, above all the Fuggerei, have benefited society. In this way, directly on site, the Fugger Foundations honor the man who had the will and the strength for this grand and timeless social endeavor.

GREEN AREA

MUSEUM IN THE AIR-RAID SHELTER

The Senior Council had the bomb shelter built in the Fuggerei in 1943, right in the middle of the Second World War. At that time, there had already been air raids on Augsburg and the underground shelter was intended to serve as a secure refuge for the residents of the Fuggerei, as well as neighbors.

Indeed, in this very shelter, 200 people survived the devastating bombing in the night of February 25th to 26th, 1944, during which 70 percent of the Fuggerei were destroyed. A total of 19 air raids on Augsburg claimed the lives of around 1,500 people, thousands were left homeless. The city center lay in dust and ashes. The Museum in the Air-Raid Shelter presents a poignant exhibition documenting the war, destruction and reconstruction of the Fuggerei and Augsburg. It is the only permanent exhibition of its kind in Bavarian Swabia.

In the shelter, the oppressive atmosphere of the war can be felt even today. A narrow staircase leads down to the former airlock which shielded against gas. From there, the path leads through six rooms featuring various audio and film stations, as well as numerous pictures, documents and original exhibits. They convey the most important events of the time, from the Nazi takeover and the war years to reconstruction.

The exhibition focuses on the Fuggerei and Augsburg – representative of many places and events of the time. Moving photos, texts and original film footage show how much the dreadful consequences of dictatorship and war changed the city and life here. But they also show how responsibility and hope for peace opened the door to a new beginning.

Opting for the future

Just a few days after the night of the bombing, the Senior Council – Joseph Ernst Fürst Fugger von Glött, Friedrich Carl Fürst Fugger-Babenhausen and Clemens Graf Fugger von Kirchberg – decided to rebuild the Fuggerei. In the middle of the war and threatened by the Nazi regime – but determined to restore the homes of the Fuggerei residents.

The Senior Council of the war and post-war years: Joseph Ernst Fürst Fugger von Glött, Friedrich Carl Fürst Fugger-Babenhausen and Clemens Graf Fugger von Kirchberg

ETERNAL, AND ALWAYS DIFFERENT

The installation "Eternity" originates from an exhibition project celebrating the 500th anniversary of the Fuggerei in 2021. In the park as well as in several flats and in the Church of St. Mark, important aspects of the foundation's core idea were displayed in an artistic setting. On the Fuggerei premises, current exhibitions are hosted frequently, such as during the annual "Lange Kunstnacht" ("Art Night") in Augsburg. During these events, the Fuggerei is presented from new perspectives. To engage in dialogue with the people of Augsburg, various events are organized on a regular basis, such as the Fugger Forum. Also the relationship with the direct neighbors in the Jakobervorstadt is promoted by our "book hut", a book swap set up in one of the Fuggerei's old wooden huts and open to everyone.

A CHURCH FOR THE FUGGEREI

When the Fuggerei was built, no one thought about a church specifically built for the housing complex, because the residents could attend mass and services at nearby churches like St. Jakob (St. Jacob's). But that changed when, in the wake of the Reformation, these churches became Protestant and were no longer an option for Catholic believers. To strengthen the Catholic faith within the Fuggerei and enable attendance of Catholic services, the administrators at the time, Markus and Philipp Eduard Fugger, had a church built on premises of the Fuggerei in 1580: St. Markus (St. Mark's).

HOORAY, IT'S SCHOOL TIME!

Towards the end of the 16th century, a school was established on the premises for children from the Fuggerei and Jakobervorstadt. The public schools were Protestant, but with its own school, the Fuggerei could provide education according to Catholic beliefs. The school comprised a teacher's flat for the schoolmaster and a classroom, which soon had to be expanded. Because back then, up to 180 children lived in the Fuggerei. Over time, the location of the school changed several times. Only after Augsburg's incorporation into the Kingdom of Bavaria in 1810, the tradition of a Fuggerei school came to an end.

AT ST. MARK'S CHURCH

Around 1600, the sacristy was established in house No. 35 next to the church, which was later converted into the sacristan's flat and school. Today, the Fuggerei pastor lives here.

Pastoral care close by

Petrus Canisius is documented as the first cleric with a direct pastoral assignment for the Fuggerei in the early 1560s. The famous Jesuit was a Cathedral preacher of Augsburg who was later canonized. At that time, masses were held in St. Mark's three times a week and on all major holidays. Initially, these masses were conducted by clerics from the Dominican monastery, starting in 1619. Since the 18th century, the Fuggerei eventually had its own chaplain, and since 1754 the Fuggerei clerics have lived directly on site.

Reliable water supply

The nostalgic pumping well in front of St. Mark's is still intact. There were several such pumping wells on the Fuggerei premises before it was connected to the water supply system. The water had to be pumped out of the ground manually, but it flowed reliably. Even when the pipeline network in Jakobervorstadt failed in 1944 due to war-related damage, the pumping wells provided the precious liquid.

CHURCH ST. MARK

Built by Hans Holl

Markus and Philipp Eduard Fugger had St. Mark's constructed by their "mason and master builder" Hans Holl, father of the famous Elias Holl. For this purpose, a brick barn, which connected the administrator's building with the houses on Herrengasse, was rebuilt in the late Renaissance style. In 1582, the modest church was consecrated in honor of the Evangelist Mark.

Architectural exception

Unlike most Catholic churches, St. Mark's does not follow the principle of orientation, that is, that the prayers are oriented towards the east. Usually, the altar faces the rising sun, which symbolizes Christ as the light of the world and the resurrection.

St. Mark's, however, was quite pragmatically designed to align with the north-south axis of Herrengasse. As a result, the choir with the altar faces south instead of east.

Use your time wisely

The sundial on the south gable was made by Carl Hermann Reusch in 1938 using the sgraffito technique; it was renewed during reconstruction. Already in the 18th century, there was a painting with a sundial and the church patron St. Mark. The saying "Nütze die Zeit" ("Use your time wisely") is often seen in connection with clocks but is also considered the motto of Jakob Fugger.

Portal with a (hi)story

An original from the late Renaissance period: the portal walls made of red marble. In contrast, the bronze bust of St. Mark dates back to 1910.

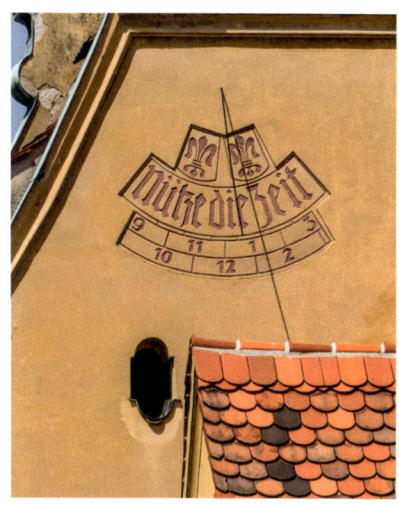

St. Mark all dressed up

In 1731, the interior of St. Mark's was remodeled in the late Baroque style, with ceiling frescoes, stucco garlands and a blue and gold canopy-like altar frame. As a result of the air raids of 1944, the church was completely destroyed by fire, only parts of the facade were still standing.

left:
The baroque interior

right:
The war-damaged facade of St. Mark's

Masterpiece St. Mark's

After the war destruction, the blessed sacristy initially served as a makeshift church from 1948 on. Two years later, the rededication of St. Mark's could be celebrated. The Senior Council had opted for an interior with a new character, reflecting the period of the church's construction. St. Mark's now features a mix of artwork from different eras.

Altar with famous painting

The carved Renaissance altar (by Wendel Dietrich) was purchased after the war and adapted to hold the existing altarpiece. The oil painting is a significant work by the Venetian artist Jacopo Palma il Giovane from around 1606. The Fugger Foundations acquired his work in 1731 in the course of the baroque redesign of the church. It was brought to safety before the air raids of 1944.

Noble wooden ceiling

Instead of a baroque sky: a noble coffered ceiling with inlaid decoration from the 16th century. It is likely, that this rarity originally came from the Fugger Foundation House near St. Anna and was acquired from private ownership in 1947. For the installation in 1949/50, wide framings had to be added. The surrounding mural paintings contain elements of the Fugger family history, such as a trident with a ring – the trade mark of the Fuggers.

Winged altar with an addition

The small, winged altarpiece (around 1550), with depictions of the Coronation of Mary, St. Michael weighing the souls and "St. Anna selbdritt" (Madonna and Child with St. Anne), used to stand in the chapel of the Fugger houses on Weinmarkt. The lower part contains a wooden panel painting which was inserted later. It depicts Markus Fugger, one of the two founders of St. Mark's, with his wife and eight children in prayer.

From the original furnishings of the late 16th century, the richly decorated sandstone baptismal font has been preserved.

Hans Leitherer's Virgin of Mercy from 1949 refers to the destruction and reconstruction of the Fuggerei.

Epitaph designed by Dürer

The epitaph for Ulrich Fugger († 1510) from the burial chapel of the Fugger family in St. Anna was heavily damaged during the Second World War. After restoration, the original made of Solnhofen Limestone was integrated into St. Mark's, while a copy can be seen in St. Anna today. The relief was designed by Albrecht Dürer and probably made by Adolf Daucher. It depicts a dead man wrapped in cloths and mourned by two satyrs. Two putti on dolphins frame the inscription.

Father Dr. Anselm Grün

DOES SPIRITUALITY REQUIRE A DEFINED FORMAT?

FATHER DR. ANSELM GRÜN

born in 1945, entered the Benedictine Abbey of Münsterschwarzach in 1964. Studied theology and obtained a doctorate on Karl Rahner's theology of the cross in 1974. Then studied business administration in Nuremberg. From 1977 to 2013, the "Cellerar", i.e., the economic director of the abbey. Author of over 300 books with a worldwide circulation of 20 million books, course instructor and spiritual director of the Recollectio House.

Spirituality means living from the spirit. Thus, it describes a mindset that is shaped by the spirit of Jesus. But spirituality requires a defined form. Those who live without form lose their vigor. Today, we have a renewed sense of rituals. Rituals give structure to the day. Rituals create a sacred time, a time that belongs to me, where I live myself instead of being lived.

Today, we are constantly exposed to external expectations – expectations from our family, from our employer, from society. Many people have the feeling that they are being dominated by these expectations. Rituals are a good counterbalance to that. It is a time that belongs to me, where I can breathe freely, where no one wants anything from me. That is good for my soul and also for my body.

God does not need our rituals. But they are good for us. They give structure to the day; they shape the day. The Greeks say: Because our life is a celebration, we shape it through rituals. I shape my day through rituals. Those who let themselves go, who live without structure, lose their inner vigor. Rituals also connect us to our roots. We often practice rituals that have been formed by our ancestors. In the Fuggerei, the residents practice the ritual of saying three prayers a day. By doing so, they partake in the faith and vitality of their ancestors. The people who have lived in the Fuggerei for 500 years have practiced this ritual in good times and bad, in times of illness and war. This has provided them with stability.

Faith needs an expression, or else it slowly dissolves. Rituals are a tangible expression of faith. In theory, we know that God is always present. But we do not live from this healing presence of God. Every day, our rituals remind us that we are carried by God's healing love, that we are not alone. And rituals give us a sense of home. We feel at home in these rituals. Because the German language knows: "Heimat" (home) is connected to "Geheimnis" (mystery). You can only be at home where the mystery lives.

> "God does not need our rituals. But they are good for us. They give structure to the day; they shape the day. The Greeks say: Because our life is a celebration, we shape it through rituals."
>
> Anselm Grün

FUTURE AND HISTORY OF THE FUGGEREI

Fuggerei NEXT500
Charter of foundation from 1521
Motivation, structure and funding
Senior council, employees and residents
The Fugger family since 1367
Jakob Fugger
Timeline History of the Fuggerei

THE FUTURE OF THE FUGGEREI: PREFERABLY ETERNALLY AND WORLDWIDE

Jubilee with a look ahead

August 23, 2021, marked the 500th anniversary of the day when Jakob Fugger issued the charter of foundation for the Fuggerei. Celebrating this special jubilee, more than a hundred events took place, ranging from exhibitions to workshops. The focus was on the core ideas of the Fuggerei as an inspiration for social housing worldwide. Because a concept that has been successful for so long could also establish a future elsewhere. Under the slogan "Fuggerei NEXT500", the Fugger Family Senior Council invited a multitude of international guests to exchange ideas about the potential of the foundation's core concept.

Signal for development

A central location for the jubilee was the temporary Fuggerei NEXT500 Pavilion at Augsburg's town hall square. For five weeks, a festival program inspired the public as well as the numerous guests who actively participated in shaping the program. For the reusable pavilion, MVRDV architects from Rotterdam used wood from the sustainably managed Fugger Foundation forests.

Pavilion interior, view of the bar

Why Fuggerei NEXT500?

500 years ago, Jakob Fugger stipulated that the Fuggerei should exist "for all eternity". His successors were tasked with doing everything necessary to ensure its continued existence and, if possible, to "increase" it – today we would use the term "develop". Additionally, Jakob Fugger built his housing complex "in exemplum", as a model or an example for others. Three good reasons for Fuggerei NEXT500. The content and goal of this concept: to further develop the mission of the Fuggerei and to make it a global model for social innovation. People and institutions all over the world can now adopt the concept of the Fuggerei Foundation and create individual "Fuggereis of the Future" in many locations. In addition, also the Fuggerei in Augsburg can and should be strengthened through endowments and donations.

The foundation stone for a "Fuggerei of the Future" in Sierra Leone has been laid: The founders Stella Rothenberger and Rugiatu Neneh Turay aim to create a sustainable social housing complex in the fishing village of Rothumba together with residents and local builders. The Fuggerei in Augsburg served as inspiration.

THE FUGGEREI CODE

Summarizing the core ideas

The concept of the Fuggerei has been adopted before, but mostly, it resulted in quite "normal" social housing complexes or housing foundations. With Fuggerei NEXT500, there now exists a kind of blueprint for housing complexes derived from the successful model of the Fuggerei. It is based on the Fuggerei's core ideas, its "secret" that sets it apart from other foundations and social housing complexes. These core ideas were first summarized in a kind of code on the occasion of the 500th anniversary of the foundation. The Fugger Code is based on a comparison of the provisions in Jakob Fugger's charter of foundation with their contemporary implementation. This has shown that there are provisions that have stood the test of time through all crises and eras because they could be adapted to the times – just like DNA or a code. They are summarized and phrased in the Code in such a way that it can serve as a blueprint or guide for the future and for other Fuggereis. For it perpetuates the core of Jakob Fugger's intention as founder, while being flexible enough for a modern and future-oriented interpretation. This allows founders to create housing foundations according to their personal goals and under their own name, which bear the hallmark of "Fuggerei" quality.

A team from the internationally renowned architectural firm MVRDV analyzed the structures of the Fuggerei and developed a modern, modular construction system based on their findings.

THE FUGGEREI CODE IN WORDING:

This site is a curated living space in perpetuity. For a minimum spiritual and monetary consideration, the foundation helps people in need in the region to lead a self-determined life in dignity. The Fuggerei concept has been setting standards since 1521.

THE MEANING OF THE INDIVIDUAL FORMULATIONS:

Living space: This is not only about accommodation. People in a Fuggerei should develop individually, but also be able to experience a sense of community.

Curated: A responsible committee implements the founder's intentions and an administration looks after the residents on site.

Perpetuity: The continued existence of a Fuggerei must be sustainably guaranteed by a forward-looking management and sufficient financial resources.

Minimum spiritual consideration: Stands for the sense of prayer or moment of calm in order to perceive one's own connection with other people.

Minimum monetary consideration: This goes back to the annual rent of one Rhenish Guilder (currently 88 cent). The consideration itself has always been important, as the residents make their own contribution and are not recipients of charity.

Foundation: A Fuggerei must be managed as a foundation

Empowers the residents: The residents should be helped to help themselves.

A life in dignity: A Fuggerei is oriented towards a life of self-determination in a good environment thanks to high-quality architecture, fittings and details.

From the region: A Fuggerei is specifically for people who have been lived in the region for a while.

Standards since 1521: The Fuggerei has set a good example in its orientation, size and quality since 1521. An example: Since the start, considerably more people in need have found a roof over their heads than in other housing foundations. One feature of a Fuggerei, therefore, is that if offers optimum space for a considerable amount of people.

Jacob van Rijs

HOW TO BUILD FOR A LIFE IN DIGNITY?

JACOB VAN RIJS

born 1964 in Amsterdam (NL), is an internationally active architect and founding partner of MVRDV – an architectural firm in Rotterdam. He is known for his daring concepts, combining bold ideas with a user-friendly focus on people. Van Rijs has led numerous of the office's most remarkable projects and is also the visionary behind the architecture of the Fuggerei NEXT500 Pavilion and the "Fuggereis of the Future".

All over the world, you can find large social housing complexes, some of which function quite well, but unfortunately, they often become so-called "problem neighborhoods". These complexes are built according to the ideal that good living conditions are a human right. Their failure often results from the sheer mass and homogeneity of the quarters and the belief that there must be a difference between social housing and housing for the rest of society. People are segregated in neighborhoods with inferior architectural quality.

This difference is rooted in the – unconscious – belief that people in social housing are somehow deserving of their fate. However, once we realize that a good education as well as loving and supportive parents with financial resources are privileges that allow socially successful people to move up the ladder – meaning that the start in life is not based on personal achievement – we can understand that living in social housing is generally not self-inflicted and therefore should not be a punishment. A "Hartz IV" (social welfare) childhood is – as ruled by the German Federal Court of Justice – not in line with human dignity.

Social housing architecture should not have less quality; rather, it should have more, as residents often live in challenging situations, and good architecture and urban planning contribute to a better quality of life. This will benefit society as a whole. Burning suburbs and "problem neighborhoods" are dreadful in every sense of the word, and they are costly and damaging to society.

What may be new is that there is now a segment of the population worldwide that is not even needy and has socially important functions, such as caregivers, police officers, firefighters, but can no longer afford housing. This is also due to the fact that in cities around the world, neighborhoods with affordable housing, the so-called Urban Villages, are either being demolished or yuppified. Therefore, the architecture and guiding principles of the Fuggerei represent an incredible innovation. From the beginning, it was designed to provide a dignified living situation for its residents with its terraced house structure, high-quality materials, community program, relatively spacious, adaptable flats and many individual features.

Of particular importance is the concept that social housing can allow people to live in dignity, and thus provide residents with the opportunity to lead a self-determined life. Housing is a human right supported by the UN and it's becoming a growing problem worldwide. We therefore need more dignified architecture for all those who can no longer afford housing as a basic necessity.

> "We therefore need more dignified architecture for all those who can no longer afford housing as a basic necessity."
>
> Jacob van Rijs

THE MOST IMPORTANT PROVISIONS IN THE CHARTER OF FOUNDATION

Valid for all eternity: The charter of foundation

Since 1521, the charter of foundation has obliged all those responsible for the Fuggerei Foundation to fulfill the intention of the founder, Jakob Fugger. The core principles of the charter, as is usually the case with any foundation, must be implemented unchanged as far as possible and in perpetuity. Therefore, in the course of 500 years, practical adjustments were made when necessary due to changing times, but nevertheless in accordance with the founder's intentions.

Provisions in the charter of foundation:

FOR ALL ETERNITY
"From now on for all eternity" … "through my cousinhood, named herein, and their descendants"

Multiple times in the charter of foundation it is mentioned that the foundation shall exist "for all eternity". Hence, Jakob Fugger had to ensure the administration of the foundations beyond his death. Since he had no children, he appointed the eldest sons of his two brothers and their descendants as administrators of the foundations. Only if there were no more surviving members of the Fugger family, the administration should to be transferred to the city of Augsburg.

RESIDENTS OF AUGSBURG IN NEED AND THEIR FAMILIES
"Poor and faithful day laborers and craftsmen that are citizens and residents of the city of Augsburg, who are indigent and devote to the most suitable"

The Fuggerei was intended for religious day laborers and craftsmen as well as their families who "are indigent" – meaning they were in need. Many craftsmen and day laborers found themselves in need during times of crisis. For these Augsburg citizens who worked or were willing to work, the Fuggerei was built. The new idea behind the Fuggerei: Thanks to affordable and good-quality housing, they would be able to lead an independent and dignified life again. Applicants had to be residents of Augsburg, but not necessarily born there.

ONE GUILDER RENT
"… each resident a guilder per year"

As a small consideration from the

Fuggerei residents, Jakob Fugger specified one guilder per year and three prayers a day. The principle of reciprocity ensured the dignity of the residents; they were not mere recipients of charity. At that time, one guilder was roughly equivalent to the weekly wage of a craftsman. Comparable flats outside the Fuggerei cost several times as much. To date, the rent has not been increased. During currency conversions, the guilder has always been converted only nominally (without taking into account the inflation rate) and is equivalent to 88 cents today.

THREE PRAYERS/CATHOLIC
"Each person, be them young or old and provided they are capable, shall say a Pater Noster, Hail Mary and the Creed every day"

It was a new approach: While in other housing foundations, people often had to pray all day, the small number of prayers required in the Fuggerei left the residents with enough time for work. It takes only a little more than a minute to recite the three prayers. Also, the residents could decide for themselves when and where they prayed. From the requirement to recite these three prayers – the Lord's Prayer, the Hail Mary and the Creed – it was later derived that Fuggerei residents must be Catholic. Although the word "Catholic" is not explicitly mentioned in the charter of foundation, the Hail Mary is only recited by Catholics, not by Lutherans or Reformists. In addition, Jakob Fugger repeatedly voiced his opposition against the emerging Reformation movement and Luther.

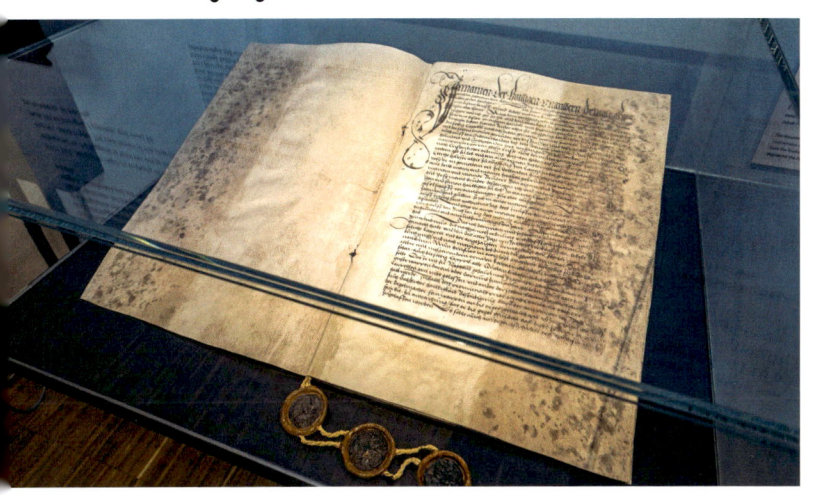

INNOVATION FUGGEREI

An exceptional housing foundation

Foundations for the benefit of needy fellow citizens were widespread in the late Middle Ages. There were alms foundations, but also housing foundations where residents lived together as a community. These housing foundations usually provided accommodation for the elderly and sick or were intended for pilgrims. The maximum number of residents was often based on a biblical number – most commonly twelve in reference to the apostles. Such housing foundations also existed in Augsburg when Jakob Fugger planned the Fuggerei. He could have simply surpassed the established models in size, but instead he developed a completely different concept.

For "Hausarme" and their families

Jakob Fugger's new concept: People in need who were capable of working should be able to live in dignity and help themselves thanks to affordable housing. So instead of the elderly and sick, he directed his efforts towards working people who needed an affordable roof over their head. In the cities, there were many so-called "Hausarme" (i.e., people who are poor although they are working and who don't go begging) who could barely afford their rent and often lived in miserable conditions. They sometimes received alms but, unlike public beggars, they were considered "humble" or "modest", and thus, honorable in their poverty. Jakob Fugger wanted to provide these fellow citizens with affordable housing so that they could get back on their feet.

Plenty of space and large flats

The sheer size of the Fuggerei was an innovation in itself at the time it was built. In Augsburg at that time, there were about 3,000 people listed in the tax records as so-called "Habnitse". "Habnitse" referred to a wealth tax category or group of people with limited financial resources who often couldn't accumulate wealth for savings and paid reduced taxes. This group of people, who were at risk of slipping into poverty in times of crisis, primarily included day laborers, construction workers and weavers. With flats for 300 people, the Fuggerei thus offered space for a relatively large number of people from this group. In addition, the flats and courtyards were also suitable for setting up a workplace. This allowed many craftsmen to work from home and not spend money on a workshop.

AUGSBURG 1521

In the year 1521, Augsburg was one of the most important economic centers in Europe, hosting major trading companies and serving as a significant political as well as cultural hub. In this metropolis lived about 30,000 people from very diverse social backgrounds. The number of citizens without any wealth constituted a significant portion of the population. Social security systems as we know them today did not exist in the 16th century. People had to build up their own savings to provide for old age and illness: With 50 guilders, one could manage to survive in old age or during times of crisis, while with 100 guilders (about two to three years' worth of a craftsman's income), one could get by more or less reasonably. Those who had less or earned nothing or very little needed support.

Social classes in Augsburg according to tax categories

approx. 50 percent:
beggars, day laborers, "Habnitse"
approx. 46 percent:
lower to upper middle class
approx. 4 percent:
financial upper class

Taxes were levied not on income but on wealth of 75 guilders or more. Those who owned less paid a head tax at most.

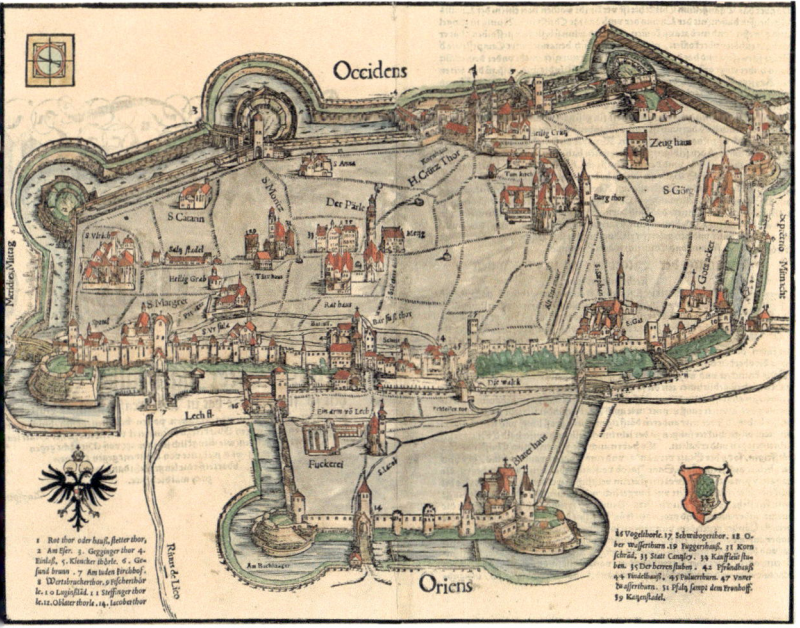

Map of Augsburg by Sebastian Münster (around 1650) with important buildings, including the Fuggerei

JAKOB FUGGER'S MOTIVATION AS A FOUNDER

Three foundations – one charter

In 1521, Jakob Fugger established his foundations also in the name of his two already deceased brothers Georg (†1506) and Ulrich (†1510). Like many other wealthy families, the Fuggers were engaged as patrons in various forms. Still during Ulrich's lifetime, it was decided to endow and build a burial chapel at St. Anna, and a separate account was set up for this purpose. In 1521, Jakob Fugger finally legally secured three foundations in a single document: the chapel at St. Anna, an endowed preachership for St. Moritz as well as the Fuggerei, which was initiated by him. The chapel endowment at St. Anna was funded with the largest sum, amounting to 15,000 guilders. But the Fuggerei in particular was unique – not only back then – due to its purpose, its scope and the amount of money Jakob Fugger provided for a housing foundation. What motivated Jacob to establish this foundation?

The portrait of Jakob Fugger bears the inscription "JACOBVS FVGGER CIVIS AVGUSTAE" (Jakob Fugger, citizen of Augsburg). The widely copied color woodcut was made by Hans Burgkmair around 1511.

Four reasons for the Fuggerei

1. Christian duty

According to the religious understanding of the time, foundations such as the Fuggerei corresponded to the Christian commandment of Caritas – charity and love of neighbor. The good deed and the prayers of the beneficiaries also contribute to the salvation of the founders and their families in the afterlife. However, for Jakob Fugger, the Fugger Foundation was not only about his salvation.

Because the Fuggerei residents were only required to recite three prayers a day, much fewer than in other housing foundations. For this purpose, he had rather intended the chapel endowment at St. Anna; he gave extensive instructions about masses and prayers that were to be held and recited there for him and his family.

2. The memory and honor of the family

Even in the late Middle Ages, it was considered just to give back to the community a portion of what one had received. "Giving" also meant increasing honor for the entire family. Honor played a very important role at that time. Founders and their families were guaranteed prestige and honor among contemporaries and even in posterity. Because foundations mean giving with lasting impact – and thus lasting honorable remembrance. This was an essential motivation for Jakob Fugger, as it was for many other founders of his time.

3. An obligation to the municipal community

People in imperial cities like Augsburg were much more bound to the system of their city than they are today. By formal admission or oath, they became members of a municipal community with its own rights, norms and duties. Jakob Fugger was part of this community: As a citizen of Augsburg, he was an equal among equals and connected with his fellow citizens in a cooperative way. It was considered a duty to take care of one another. With the Fuggerei Foundation, Jakob Fugger also wanted to take responsibility and help fellow citizens in need.

4. Creative drive and ambition

In addition to religious and social motivation, Jakob Fugger's personal traits, in particular his creative drive, also played a role: He wanted to improve help for the poor, making it long-lasting and more effective than before. His new approach: People in need who are capable of working should be able to live in dignity and help themselves thanks to affordable housing. Also new: size and layout of the housing complex, which allowed for a self-determined life.

NINE ACTIVE FOUNDATIONS

Reorganization under Anton Fugger

As the nephew and successor of Jakob Fugger, Anton Fugger successfully continued to run the family business and also the foundations. In 1548, he restructured the existing three foundations based on Jakob's charter of foundation and revised some provisions. Also, Anton established additional foundations under the same umbrella. Today, there are nine Fugger Foundations that have existed without interruption since the 16th century and are managed collectively.

Anton Fugger, Portrait by Hans Maler from Schwaz

Burial chapel at St. Anna

The Fugger burial chapel served as a memorial for the deceased members of the family and for representation purposes. Not only the brothers Georg, Ulrich and Jakob rest in the crypt, but also Jakob's nephews Hieronymus and Raymund Fugger. The foundation finances the preservation of the Catholic chapel in the now Protestant church of St. Anna.

Predicant office at St. Moritz

Jakob Fugger belonged to the congregation of St. Moritz and was engaged to improve the quality of preaching. In 1517, the Pope granted him the right to henceforth choose a theologian for the preacher's post. He ensured the funding of the post with the foundation of the predicant office. The "right of presentation" is still exercised by the Family Senior Council to this day.

Fuggerei

A contract with the city of Augsburg in 1516 laid down the fundamental aspects of the housing complex that was to be built. In 1523, while Jakob Fugger was still alive, the Fuggerei was completed with 52 planned houses. As Jakob's successor, Anton Fugger complemented the complex and managed its maintenance.

Wood and Pox House ("Holz- und Blatternhaus")

The "Holz- und Blatternhaus" in the Fuggerei was put into operation as early as the 1520s. In 1548 it was made into an independent foundation by Anton Fugger.

Veit Hörl Foundation

Veit Hörl, a mercantile servant of the Fuggers, provided foundation capital for charitable purposes in his 1546 will. Accordingly, in 1548, Anton Fugger established an endowment to the Wood and Pox House ("Holz- und Blatternhaus"), which allowed for the treatment of more patients.

Infirmary Waltenhausen

In 1537, Jakob Fugger's nephew, Hieronymus Fugger, bequeathed capital in his will to establish a facility to support impoverished servants of the Fuggers as well as family members in need. The charter of foundation was written in 1548.

Dr. Simon Scheibenhardt Foundation

Dr. Simon Scheibenhardt served as a preacher at St. Moritz, starting in 1555. In his 1567 will, he designated a foundation for the benefit of the poor and sick of Catholic faith.

Surgical Hospital ("Schneidhaus")

In 1560, just a few weeks before his death, Anton Fugger added an amendment to his will, establishing a foundation for the treatment of the needy by surgeons and wound doctors in the "Schneidhaus", a surgical facility near the Fuggerei.

Dr. Johannes Mylius Foundation

The scholarship foundation, established in 1595 through the will of a legal representative of the Fuggers in Spain, enabled the establishment of a college with places for tuition-free studies in the now-Belgian city of Leuven.

WELL-INVESTED MONEY

The funding of the Fuggerei

The Fuggerei is funded by a separate, independent and charitable foundation with its own resources, which may only be used for the foundation's purpose. The financial origins of the foundation trace back to a sum of 30,000 guilders provided by Ulrich Fugger. In the year 1511, there were still 15,000 guilders left. Since then, the funds were managed via the "St. Ulrich Account", which was established for charitable purposes, following the example of Italian merchants. This purpose is also indicated by the naming after a saint. Additionally, Jakob contributed money from his private means to fund the construction of the Fugger Chapel at St. Anna and the Fuggerei. In the charter of foundation from 1521, he established the financial basis with an additional 10,000 guilders and outlined the framework for the future use of the foundation funds. The foundation capital was invested at the standard interest rate of 5 percent, and the investment income was used for the expenses of the foundations, such as the maintenance of the Fuggerei.

From capital to real estate

In 1548, Anton Fugger separated the financial administration of the foundations from the trading business. This ensured their economic independence and continued existence regardless of the Fugger's trading company. In 1660, another decisive step was taken: After capital investments proved to be insecure during the Thirty Years' War, the foundation funds were now invested in real estate. In retrospect, this transformation from a capital foundation to a real estate foundation was forward-thinking. The proceeds from real estate and forestry properties ensured the survival of the Fugger family even in times of inflation and currency reforms.

The basis: The Foundation Forests

The Fugger Foundations, including the Fuggerei, are still primarily financed through the proceeds from the forestry operations. 3,200 hectares of forest land are owned by the foundations. For generations, efforts have been made to maintain and develop these forests into stable mixed stands to ensure the forest's resilience for the future. The proportion of spruce trees has already been reduced to 64 percent.

Important:
Admissions and donations

In addition to forestry, the admission fees from Fuggerei visitors make a significant contribution to the preservation of the Fuggerei. Also, in the anniversary year 2021, the "Fuggerei Förderstiftung" was established. In this way, the foundation's purpose can be supported easily and securely through donations and contributions.

Maintenance, modernization and administration of the Fuggerei have always been financed through foundation assets – without any funding or subsidies from the government. The Fuggerei flats are continuously being renovated, with a focus on making them as accessible as possible. For this purpose, around 60,000 euros need to be invested per flat.

The Fugger Foundation Forest

THE WORK OF MANY GENERATIONS

Honorary responsibility for the foundations

Jakob Fugger's marriage remained childless. In his wills, he designated the descendants of his brothers Georg and Ulrich to be responsible for the foundations as long as their lineages exist. Jakob's nephew, Anton Fugger, had already set the course for the foundations through some fundamental decisions. Over the centuries, his successors managed to navigate the Fuggerei through economic and political crises, rebuild it after destruction and also adapt it to the times. Only in this way is it possible to fulfill the foundation's purpose of being a home for the needy "for all eternity". This provision in the charter of foundation is an obligation for Jakob Fugger's successors to follow in his footsteps and explore innovative paths to ensure the continued existence of the Fuggerei.

Responsible for the foundations today

From the circle of individuals defined by Jakob Fugger as responsible for the foundations, three lineages exist today. They go back to Anton and Raymund Fugger, both sons of his brother Georg. Each lineage appoints a member to the "Fürstlich und Gräflich Fuggersches Familienseniorat" (i.e., the full title of the Fugger Family Senior Council), traditionally the head of the respective lineage. Today, other representatives of the lineages also take on this responsibility. The Family Senior Council, serving on an honorary and economically independent basis, functions as a strategic decision-making level for the Fugger Foundations. In legal terms, it is the organ of the foundations and thus their legal representative.

In today's Fugger Family Senior Council, the 16th generation since Jakob Fugger and his brothers is active:

- **Alexander Erbgraf Fugger-Babenhausen** (Chairman of the Senior Council) from the lineage Fugger-Babenhausen
- **Maria Theresia Gräfin Fugger von Glött** from the lineage Fugger von Glött
- **Isabella Gräfin Thun-Hohenstein** from the lineage Fugger-Kirchberg
- **Leopold Graf Fugger-Babenhausen** from the lineage Fugger-Babenhausen (advisory member)

Isabella Gräfin Thun-Hohenstein, Alexander Graf Fugger-Babenhausen, Leopold Graf Fugger-Babenhausen and Theresia Gräfin Fugger von Glött (from left to right) welcome Rip Rapson (center), CEO of the US-based Kresge Foundation, at the Senior Council building in the Fuggerei.

The traditionally close exchange with associations, institutions and foundations around the world is crucial for the further development of the Fuggerei. Concepts like Fuggerei NEXT500 demonstrate that the core idea of the Fuggerei can also provide solutions to global challenges.

The Senior Council is organized in such a way that decisions are made through the collaboration of all Fugger lineages. The members of the Senior Council are also called "Senioren" or "Konsenioren". Every four years, they elect or confirm a chairman or chairwoman who presides over the meetings and serves as the primary point of contact for administration and the public. Nevertheless, all members of the Senior Council assume representative duties and maintain close communication with each other and with the administration.

The responsibilities of the Senior Council include:

- Decisions regarding the interpretation of the foundation's charter
- Fundamental decisions regarding the development of the Fuggerei, such as long-term financing, personnel, public relations and tourism-related matters
- Representation to the public, politics, authorities and media
- Legal representation of the foundation

TOGETHER FOR A VALUABLE GOAL

The administration

The administration professionals manage the foundation's properties, which enable the maintenance of the Fuggerei, and oversee all aspects of day-to-day operations: the management of the Fuggerei flats and the concerns of the residents, the constructional development of the Fuggerei, public relations, all foundation-related matters, such as dealing with authorities, the Church, the Fugger Archives and the Foundation Forest Office, but also financial accounting and personnel planning. Around 50 people from various professions work for the Fuggerei.

The head of the Fuggerei administration is the administrator. He bears the executive responsibility for the Fuggerei and maintains close communication with the Senior Council. Among his core responsibilities is financial and asset management, including budget responsibility for all operational measures. The administrator is involved in the day-to-day operations on site and assumes the duties of a managing director. He also serves as a representative of the Fuggerei to the public and associations.

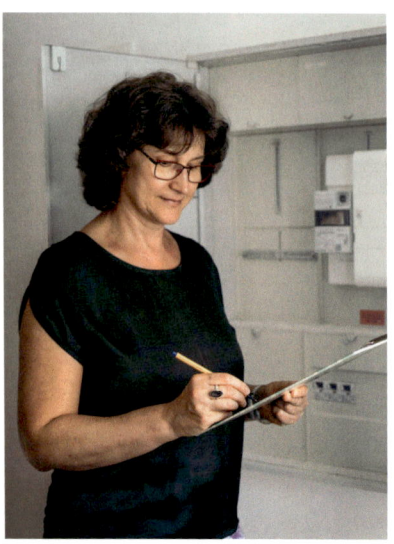

Administrator Wolf-Dietrich Graf von Hundt heads the administration. Additionally, he serves as a kind of mayor for important concerns of the residents.

The Fuggerei pastor

Traditionally, the Fuggerei has its own pastor, who also resides there. He attends to pastoral care, conducts the services at St. Mark's and administers the sacraments when requested. For their pastor, the residents pay the same contribution as they do for their rent: 88 cents annually.

The Archives

The Fugger Archives ("Fürstlich und Gräflich Fuggersches Familien- und Stiftungsarchiv") is located in Dillingen an der Donau. There, the archivist and his team manage the historical records of the different Fugger family lineages and the foundations, respond to inquiries and assist archive users. Responsible for the overall coordination of research is the Scientific Director of the Fugger Archives.

Forestry

Responsible for the sustainable management of the foundation's forests are the Foundation Forestry Office in Laugna and several forestry bureaus. Since the 19th century, the foundations have relied on personnel with forestry expertise for this purpose. This has fostered a strong forest conservation mindset and strategic, long-term thinking for the forestry operation. Today, 15 employees manage the foundations' approximately 3,200 hectares of forest land, balancing economic, ecological and social aspects.

THE ADMISSION PROCEDURE

FINDING A HOME IN THE FUGGEREI

Enough room for a life in dignity

The waiting list for a Fuggerei flat is currently 104 requests long. The number of applications has increased significantly. The main causes are rising rents, but also new life situations in which the income is no longer sufficient for housing. With an annual "cold" rent (i.e., not including utility bills) of only 88 cents in the Fuggerei, at least a significant part of the financial worries is alleviated. This allows many residents to lead a life in dignity that is more than just the daily struggle for existence.

Overview of admission criteria

The provisions in the 1521 charter of foundation are still valid today. However, the interpretation of the regulations does not rigidly adhere to that of the 16th century but has been continually adapted to the times. This also applies to the requirements that applicants for a Fuggerei flat must meet:

AUGSBURGER CITIZEN: Applicants must have lived in the city of Augsburg for the last 2 years.

CATHOLIC: Applicants must be registered with the Catholic parish responsible for their place of residence.

BEING IN NEED: Certain income and property thresholds must not be exceeded.

ADDITIONALLY:

RESPECTABLE: Applicants must provide a Criminal Records Bureau disclosure as proof of no previous convictions.

INDEPENDENT HOUSEKEEPING:
Applicants shall be able to keep house with no further assistance.

IMPORTANT: Age or marital status is not a relevant admission criterion. Persons of all ages and marital status, singles, married couples, divorcés and divorcées, families as well as single parents with their children can apply.

The application process: personal and confidential

The allocation of a Fuggerei flat follows clear, transparent rules. Throughout the entire process, all reports and data are subject to strict confidentiality. Applicants have their initial interviews with one of the two social workers to address personal concerns and questions, as well as formalities. If all admission criteria are met and all necessary data and documents are provided, the waiting period begins. Depending on desired flat, urgency of the application and length of the waiting list, this can take around three to five years. As soon as a suitable flat becomes available and the applicant is interested in it, the administrator receives a report from the social worker. The applicant then has an interview with the social worker and the administrator together. Afterwards, the administrator submits the application for a decision to the representative of the Fugger lineage responsible for the current application since this task alternates between the Fugger lineages. If the admission is approved, the applicant is granted the right of residence. Before moving in, the foundation and the resident sign a rental agreement, which also includes the acknowledgement of the special house rules in the Fuggerei.

Helping people help themselves

The right of residence in the Fuggerei is granted for life. But it is also a tool for self-help. The security of affordable rent often helps to overcome personal or financial crises. There are no rent increases, at most, costs for electricity and heating may increase. In addition, all residents who wish to do so are assisted in finding a job or acquiring qualifications. When their circumstances improve, residents also move out. For example: residents in training or retraining who couldn't afford another flat for a while.

CURRENT DEVELOPMENTS

Today, the largest group of applicants is no longer retirees, but single parents, low-income workers and people with interrupted work histories. One to two-thirds of the residents are employed full-time or part-time. Some residents work in the Fuggerei on an hourly basis as night guard, cashier or sacristan. Others are actively engaged in voluntary work, either within the Fuggerei itself or in social institutions.

A FORTUNATE START IN THE CITY

The Fuggers from 1367 until today

"Fucker advenit, dedit XLIIII den. Dignus." reads a line in the Augsburg tax records of 1367: "Fugger has arrived, gave 44 pfennige, he is worthy."

The mentioned "Fugger" was Hans Fugger, a weaver from the Augsburg region who wanted to make his fortune in the city. For this, he brought starting capital, as evidenced by the aforementioned tax of 44 pfennige. So, the first Fugger in Augsburg was not destitute, as is often stated. The addition "he is worthy" meant that he was qualified to receive citizenship. Hans Fugger soon acquired his citizenship through his marriage with Clara Widolf, the daughter of a master weaver. After her death, he married Elisabeth Gfattermann, who also came from a weaver family. Hans Fugger was not only involved in weaving but also succeeded in the cloth trade. By 1396, he was already ranked 40th among the taxpayers in Augsburg.

The next generation: Successful with overseas trade

When Hans Fugger passed away in 1408, Elisabeth continued to manage the business for their underage sons, Andreas and Jakob, and increased the wealth left behind. The brothers both learned the goldsmith trade before joining their parents' overseas trade. After their mother's death in 1436, they parted ways. The business and wealth of Jakob Fugger the Elder flourished. When he died in 1469, his widow Barbara Bäsinger successfully continued the overseas trade in goods such as cotton, wool, silk and tropical fruits. Like her mother-in-law, she outlived her husband by 28 years. Together with her children, she strengthened the family's business and reputation. In 1473, the family received the Lily Coat of Arms. The youngest son was 14 years old at the time and bore his father's name – he would later become known as Jakob Fugger the Rich.

Networked entrepreneurs: Ulrich, Georg and Jakob Fugger

In 1494, the brothers Ulrich, Georg and Jakob Fugger entered into a partnership agreement. They divided the responsibilities and tasks within the company and rose to become leading merchants of their time by combining trade in precious metals and commodities with financing activities. The brothers established a network of significant clients and branches in central European cities. After the deaths of Georg and Ulrich, Jakob Fugger became the sole leader of the company. Since his marriage remained childless, he designated his nephews as his successors in his will. After Jakob's death in 1525, his nephew Anton successfully ran the company.

From merchants to noblemen

With the proceeds from trade, three generations acquired extensive real and manorial property until the 17th century, which became the new economic and social foundation of the family. Around 1650, more than 280 years after Hans Fugger's arrival in Augsburg, the company ceased operations. Merchants had become nobles who gained important positions in the Church and the Empire. With a portion of their wealth, the Fugger family established independent foundations, the continuity of which they oversee to this day. They also played a significant role in patronage of music, art and literature, as well as the preservation and maintenance of family estates and castles. The coat of arms of the "Fugger von der Lilie" ("Fuggers of the Lily") can be found in many places in Swabia, where the three Fugger families are still based today: Grafen Fugger-Kirchberg in castle Oberkirchberg near Ulm, Fürsten Fugger von Glött at castle Kirchheim and Fürsten Fugger-Babenhausen at castle Babenhausen and castle Wellenburg near Augsburg.

Depiction of the family's coat of arms in the "Fugger Book of Honor" ("Ehrenbuch der Fugger"), which dates back to the mid-16th century.

LIFE AND WORK

Apprenticeship in Italy

Jakob Fugger was born on March 6, 1459, as the tenth of eleven children into the successful merchant family. At the age of twelve, he already held an ecclesiastical benefice (a church office associated with income) at Herrieden Monastery. However, he did not pursue studies or receive the higher orders. An ecclesiastical career, as often told, was probably not intended for Jakob after all. Rather, he went to Venice at the age of 14. Here, he acquired the skills and knowledge for his future success. In 1487, he returned to Augsburg.

A new era for the company

Under his older brothers Ulrich and Georg, the company was already trading in copper and silver and was also active in the credit business. After Jakob's return, however, the business volume increased significantly. Like other merchants of the time, the Fuggers secured their loans to rulers and institutions with rights, such as in trade and ore mining. With this strategy, Jakob brought the Fugger company to the forefront of European credit and trading houses. Due to their financial strength, the Fuggers became one of the most important financiers for the House of Habsburg, especially for the future Emperor Maximilian I. After 1510, as the sole "Regierer und Schaffierer" (leader) of the company, Jakob significantly increased both business and profits. His success was closely linked to an innovative communication network. Thanks to the company's trading posts all over Europe, news traveled fast and regularly to his Augsburg office, such as information on exchange rates and financial transactions, as well as political and economic developments. Jakob leveraged this information edge for his decision-making and also strategically for maintaining customer relations.

Rising in society

In 1498, Jakob married the young Sibylla Artzt. Thanks to her patrician status, Jakob now belonged to the social class of the "Mehrer" (literally: enhancers). This gave him access to the so-called "Herrenstube", although the Fuggers still did not belong to the patriciate. In 1514, he was granted the title of a Reichsgraf (Imperial Count); yet he continued to refer to himself as a "citizen of Augsburg" until his death. Jakob and Sybilla shone as hosts at numerous festivities. The Fugger Palace on today's Maximilianstraße was open to the Emperor or important emissaries during their visits to Augsburg.

The imperial election

Jakob Fugger remained closely associated with Emperor Maximilian I until his death in 1519. For Maximilian's grandson and successor, Charles of Spain, Jakob secured the election as Emperor. Charles was in competition with the French king and the English king during this time. For their votes, the Electors demanded the exorbitant sum of 851,918 guilders, of which Jakob Fugger provided nearly two-thirds, while the Welser family, along with Genoese banks, covered the rest.

"Use your time wisely"

In 1521, Augsburg was suffering from a wave of the plague. Perhaps this is why Jakob Fugger thought the time had come to secure the foundations. Furthermore, he had been in poor health for a while. He had a leg ulcer, and it was anticipated that he would not live for very long. At the age of 66, he died of an abdominal ulcer on December 30, 1525. Even on his deathbed, he was still working.

The wedding picture by Hans Burgkmair: The 19-year-old Sybilla adorned with rich jewelry and holding a sheet of music, indicating her love for music. Jakob Fugger, 20 years older, wears a golden cap, as did many merchants who had a close personal connection to Venice.

CRITICISM AND LEGENDS

The imperial election is one of the topics that contributed to the legend-building and critical examination of Jakob Fugger. Even during his lifetime, his name was synonymous with wealth and influence. A Portuguese envoy even referred to him as the most important man in Germany. Jakob leveraged the political circumstances of his time, and in turn, he was utilized for political ends. The notion that he was the richest man in world history is one of many Fugger legends. There have been and are wealthier people, in terms of the conversion value of his wealth to today's gold prices as well as other comparative values. A definite superlative, however, is Jakob's foundations, especially the Fuggerei.

FROM 1514

A BRIEF HISTORY OF THE FUGGEREI AND THE FUGGER FOUNDATIONS

1514 Jakob Fugger purchases properties in the quarter Jakobervorstadt to provide housing for Augsburg citizens who are in need but willing to work.

1516 Agreement with the city of Augsburg to regulate the taxation for the future Fuggerei. In this agreement, the yearly rent of one Rhenish Guilder is set as well.

August 23, 1521 In the charter of foundation, Jakob Fugger legally secures the Fuggerei, the burial chapel at St. Anna and the predicant office at St. Moritz. This day is regarded as the founding date of the three foundations.

1523 Completion of the Fuggerei with 52 houses.

30th of December 1525 Jakob Fugger dies. His nephew Anton succeeds him as director of the Fugger business.

1548 Anton Fugger restructures the foundations. Additional foundations are established by the end of the century.

1582 The residents of the Fuggerei receive their own Catholic church: St. Mark's.

1592 Beginning of schooling in the Fuggerei, with the school remaining until around 1810.

1632–1635 During the Thirty Years' War, the Fuggerei is occupied by Swedish troops for some time. The residents are displaced, but later return to their destroyed houses. They partly repair the war damages themselves, as the foundations are facing financial problems due to defaulting interest payments.

1660 Due to the repayment of a 60,000 guilder loan from 1586, the Fugger Foundations are able to purchase property. This marks the transformation from capital-based foundations to property-based foundations.

1806 The sovereign rights as well as the legal rights of the Fugger assets fall to the Kingdom of Bavaria. However, the Fugger family

TO THE FUTURE

contractually manage to secure their decision-making authority in regard to the foundations and thus prevent the confiscation of the foundations' assets.

19th century
Through sustainable and professional management, the forest becomes the main source of income for the Fugger Foundations.

End of the 19th century
Increasing number of applications for Fuggerei flats. At the end of the century, the waiting time is about 15 to 18 years.

1923
Due to currency devaluation (hyperinflation), many foundations suffer financial losses. Being property-based, the Fugger Foundations are less affected by this phenomenon.

After 1933
Foundations and charities see themselves threatened with incorporation into Nazi-organisations. The Fugger Foundations as well were in danger of losing their independence.

1943
An air-raid shelter is built at the Fuggerei. During the air strikes on the 25th/26th of February 1944, 750 people die and 80,000 lose their homes. Three quarters of the Fuggerei are destroyed. Most residents need to be evacuated. Only three days later, on the 1st of March 1944, the Fugger Senior Council decides to rebuild the Fuggerei.

Starting in 1945:
Reconstruction of the Fuggerei and acquisition of properties for its expansion. In 1947, the first of the damaged houses are restored and evacuated residents return. New admissions are also resumed again.

1973
The expansion of the Fuggerei to now 140 flats in 67 houses is completed.

2021
Celebration of the 500th anniversary of the foundation. The concept of "Fuggerei NEXT500" thinks into the future: More Fuggereis can be created internationally – individually adapted to the specific local needs. Founders all over the world are welcome to join this idea.

PHOTO CREDITS

Astrid Förster   **page 21**
Augsburger Allgemeine, Photo: Paul Engert   **page 30, 65**
Barbra Verbij   **page 88**
Bayerische Staatsbibliothek, Cgm 9460   **page 107**
Bayerisches Landesamt für Denkmalpflege, Photo: Carl Stechele   **page 57**
Bayerisches Landesamt für Denkmalpflege, Photo: Gröber   **page 39**
Bayerisches Landesamt für Denkmalpflege   **page 16, 20, 56**
Fugger-Archives, Photo: Agathe Bunz   **page 28, 30**
Fugger-Archives, Photo: Erika Groth-Schmachtenberger   **page 68**
Fugger-Archives, Photo: Ingeborg Thal   **page 47**
Fugger-Archives, Weidenbacher (1926)   **page 46**
Fugger-Archives, Wolfgang Kilian, Stadtplan Augsburg (1626)   **page 49**
Fugger-Archives   **page 56, 71, 77**
Fugger Foundation, Photo: Daniel Biskup   **page 22, 29, 31, 36, 39, 51, 75, 99, 103**
Fugger Foundation, Photo: Eckhart Matthäus (title, collapse)   **page 12-18,
20-21, 25, 27, 34-50, 54, 57-61, 63, 68-70, 74-79, 91**   Hans Burgkmair (approx. 1511)   **page 94**
Fugger Foundation, Illustrator: Jonas Lauströer   **page 37**
Fugger Foundation, Photo: Nikky Meier   **page 18, 60, 72-73, 84**
Fugger Foundation, Photo: Oliver Soulas
page 3-4, 26, 28, 31, 50, 52, 61-62, 64, 68, 84, 101-103, 105
Fugger Foundation, Photo: Quirin Leppert   **page 24, 82, 85-86**
Fugger Foundation   **page 10, 18-19, 27, 50, 56, 65, 73, 99**
Heiß, Wien / altaugsburggesellschaft   **page 27**
Kunstsammlungen und Museen Augsburg, Jörg Seld, Stadtplan Augsburg (1521)   **page 9**
Museum of Applied Art Budapest, Johann Schrettegger, Sonnenuhr (18. Jh.)   **page 41**
PfefferminzGreen e.V.   **page 85**
Private collection   **page 108**
Reichsstädtische Bibliothek Lindau, Caspar Stromayr, Practica Copiosa (1559)   **page 97**
SLUB Dresden/Map collection, (Sebastian Münster), Vogelschaubild Augsburg (1650)   **page 93**
Staatliche Kunsthalle Karlsruhe, Hans Maler zu Schwaz (1525)   **page 96**
Augsburg City Archive   **page 19, 106**
Augsburg University Library, Photo: Erika Groth-Schmachtenberger   **page 31**

We would like to thank all those who provided images and everyone who supported the creation of this guide with their feedback and information.